# HOME
# IMPROVEMENTS

Also by R. Dodge Woodson:

*The Complete Guide to Buying Your First Home*
*The Complete Guide to Home Plumbing Repair and Replacement*
*Get the Most for Your Remodeling Dollar*
*Rehab Your Way to Riches*

# HOME IMPROVEMENTS

## Making investments in your home that pay for themselves

R. DODGE WOODSON

BETTERWAY BOOKS
CINCINNATI, OHIO

Typography by Park Lane Production Services

97 96 95 94 93    5 4 3 2 1

**Library of Congress Cataloging-in-Publication Data**

Woodson, R. Dodge (Roger Dodge)
    Home improvements: making investments in your home that pay for themselves / by R. Dodge Woodson.
        p. cm.
    Includes index.
    ISBN 1-55870-303-9
    1. Dwellings--Remodeling--Costs. 2. Dwellings--Remodeling--Cost effectiveness. 3. Real estate investment. I. Title.
TH4816.W633 1993
643'.7'0299--dc20                         93-24793
                                          CIP

*This book is dedicated to my daughter, Afton, and my wife, Kimberley. Their love and encouragement keeps me writing. These ladies of my life are my life.*

# ACKNOWLEDGMENTS

I would like to acknowledge my parents, Maralou and Woody, for all the help they have given me over the years. Thanks, Mom and Dad.

Jane L. Furbeck-Owen is licensed as a Certified General Appraiser in the state of Maine, and she provided professional opinions for many of the projects discussed throughout this book. Jane is a general partner in Brunswick Real Estate Services, a Brunswick, Maine, appraisal firm. I would like to thank Jane for adding an extra dimension to this book.

The following companies were kind enough to provide illustrations for this book, and I would like to acknowledge and thank them:

Azrock Floor Products
Congoleum Corporation
Lis King Public Relations
Mannington Resilient Floors
Quaker Maid
U.S. Department of Agriculture
Velux-America, Inc.
Weil-McLain, a division of The Marley Co.
Wood-Mode, Inc.

# CONTENTS

# INTRODUCTION

If you are thinking of investing in home improvements, you should not buy *anything* until you read this book. What makes this book so important to your purchase of home improvements? The information between these pages exposes facts about costs and values that most people never know until they have lost money. Since most people don't like to lose money, this book should be considered the foundation of your plans for any type of home improvement.

Are you thinking of landscaping your front lawn? If you are, the details of greatest interest to you are in Chapter Two.

Have you always wondered what room holds the most profit potential for home improvements? If you have, Chapters Twelve and Thirteen will prove interesting reading.

Regardless of whether your plans call for build- ing a deck, remodeling your kitchen, or replacing your old heating system, you will find facts and figures here to help in your planning and budgeting.

What makes this book different from other books on similar subjects? This book gives you reader-friendly information that is not one-sided. You will see the costs and values of various home improvements from the perspectives of a licensed real estate appraiser, a licensed real estate broker, a licensed general contractor, and a master plumber. You will also be given historical statistics and information from other sources.

The author's conversational writing style is designed to make this book enjoyable to read, so you will not feel as though you are sifting through pages of lifeless cost estimates. The pace is fast, and the facts may surprise you. This book should be read by anyone intending to invest in home improvements.

## How to Use this Book

Knowing how to use this book will make the contents more valuable to you. There are no secret codes to learn or complicated construction terms to figure out, but if you have a question on the meaning of a word, there is a Glossary at the back of the book for your convenience.

The subject of this book is defining the value of home improvements. Value is not always the same as price. For example, you may pay $25,000 for a swimming pool that two weeks later has a value of only $12,000.

Some home improvements are like new cars: they are expensive to buy, but if you try to sell them after a few weeks, they are no longer worth nearly what you paid for them. This may be acceptable for an improvement that cost a couple hundred dollars, but if you spend thousands of dollars, you cannot afford to take such a loss. Luckily, this book is going to help you avoid financial disasters.

Are there any types of home improvements that may be worth more than they cost? Yes, some types of improvements can indeed be worth more than their initial cost. Kitchens and bathrooms offer some of the best potential for strong returns on improvement investments.

As you read through the chapters that follow, you will see three sets of numbers for most jobs. The first figure represents the estimated cost of a job when the homeowner provides all of the labor required.

Some homeowners lack the skills or desire to hammer nails and solder pipes. For these homeowners, the second figure in the comparisons represents the estimated costs of jobs where the homeowner acts as a general contractor but does none of the physical work.

The third figure given in many examples represents the probable cost of the jobs when a professional general contractor is retained.

While the thrust of this book is costs and values, it is also filled with tips for do-it-yourselfers. Many jobs can be accomplished by the average homeowner, but some types of work are best left to professionals. You will find advice sprinkled throughout the examples that tells you when professional help should be given serious consideration.

One of the most important steps in avoiding financial losses from home improvements is proper planning. Chapter One instructs you in professional methods for assessing home improvement values. After reading this chapter, you will know how real estate appraisers do their jobs and how their techniques can affect the value of your home improvements.

A quick glance at the table of contents will show you where to look for general types of improvements, and the index will help you find specific projects of interest.

As you evaluate the projects discussed in this book, it is important for you to understand that the figures given may not be representative of costs and values for your particular home. Real estate values can fluctuate greatly from neighborhood to neighborhood, from state to state. The economic climate of the area where you live has a tremendous effect on housing values.

The estimates in this book give you good examples of how costs and values relate to each other with various types of improvements, but the exact figures may differ in your area. Before you make a buying decision, follow the advice given in the book for conducting your own research and price evaluation.

# ASSESSING HOME IMPROVEMENT VALUES

Assessing home improvement values may be more important now than it has ever been before. Of course, determining the value of what you are paying for is always important, but due to the present real estate cycle, the cost and value of home improvements deserve some extra attention.

There are many reasons for investing in home improvements. Some people improve their homes to make living conditions more enjoyable. During bad economic times, people turn to home improvements as an alternative to buying a larger, different, or new home. And some people are forced to use home improvements as an enticement for buyers when a home must be sold. All of these are viable reasons for spending money to improve your home. The question is, are you getting your money's worth? This book is going to help you make wise buying decisions and show you how to evaluate various forms of popular home improvements.

## DETERMINING THE VALUE OF HOME IMPROVEMENTS

How you determine the value of your improvements will depend, to a large extent, on why you are making the improvement. For example, if you are improving your home with the sole intent of selling the house, you cannot use the same evaluation techniques that might be employed on improvements purely for personal enjoyment. If you are installing replacement windows to reduce your annual utility costs, you will have to assess how long you must live

in the house to recover your investment. Should you decide to install a swimming pool, you must be prepared for the fact that you may recover less than half of your investment when the property is sold.

Home improvements can also be used to build equity in your home. Just by working around the house on weekends, you can build significant equity in your residence. This equity can be used to extend your borrowing power for the education of your child or for that new boat you have always wanted. To make the most of equity-building improvements, you must take an active role in the job. You might do the job yourself, or you may act as a general contractor; either way, you can build equity in your home.

As you can see, there are many reasons for considering the improvement of your home. There are also many ways to assess the value of those improvements, and that is what we are going to discuss throughout this book.

You will be given advice from all sides of the issue. You will hear it from the position of a real estate appraiser, a real estate broker, a remodeling contractor, and experts in other fields. In general, you will receive a well-rounded and complete education in evaluating home improvements. Now, if you are ready, let's begin.

## VALUE CATEGORIES

There are several different categories to consider when placing a value on an intended home improvement. Before we look at the different ways to determine values, let's look at some examples of the various categories of home improvements.

## Personal Enjoyment

Personal enjoyment is one common reason for making improvements to your home. However, improvements that are of high personal value may not fare too well in terms of resale value. When you make these improvements, you must be aware that the money invested in the improvement may not be recovered when your home is sold.

What types of home improvements fall into this category? There are so many possibilities, it is really up to the homeowner. Some common examples could include:

- swimming pools
- tennis courts
- lavish backyard gardens
- ornamental fish ponds
- saunas
- spas
- privacy fencing

Of course, this is only a small assortment of the improvements that could fall into the personal enjoyment category.

Putting a value on improvements made with the sole purpose of bringing happiness to a homeowner is very difficult. It is easy to determine how much a whirlpool spa will cost, and there are logical ways to assess the spa's value at the time of resale. However, deciding on a value to the individual using the spa is not so easy.

A spa that costs $1,500 may be worth $1,500 to one person, $500 to another person, and $2,500 to someone else. Since personal enjoyment values are intangible, we will not attempt to put a price tag on them. We will, however, look at acquisition costs and market values.

## Functional Improvements

Functional improvements are improvements made to improve the use of a property. For example, a four-bedroom house that has only one bathroom is not very functional. Adding a second bathroom to the house would improve its usefulness and probably its market value.

Functional improvements can also serve as personal enjoyment improvements, but they are not always in the same category. For example, an expanding family might need to convert their attic to living space. While the additional living space makes its home more functional and is certainly enjoyed, the improvement may not be an investment the family has dreamed of making. Adding an extra bedroom is rarely as exciting as adding a swimming pool. It may be needed more, and it may make life in the home more enjoyable, but it is not quite a personal enjoyment improvement.

## Equity

Some money-conscious homeowners improve their homes to increase their equity position. The improvements made for this reason are normally logical, functional, and well-researched.

The expanding family who adds a bedroom out of necessity may be increasing their equity in the home, but money will not be their motivation for the additional living space. However, the handy couple who can work a little on the weekends to finish their basement into living space or convert their attic into a studio loft may be doing so for money. They probably won't be putting cash in their pockets immediately, but they will be building equity that will help them in the future.

## Sales Incentive

There are times in the real estate market when improvements are a necessary sales incentive. If you were trying to sell your house and all the prospective buyers were complaining about the ugly carpet, you might have to replace the carpet to attract a willing buyer.

Improvements made as sales incentives can be risky. Making the wrong improvements or paying too much for the improvements can worsen an already bad situation. All types of improvements should be weighed carefully, but this type should command strong attention.

Your best resource for determining the right improvements to make as sales incentives is a good real estate broker. He or she can quickly and tactfully advise you that replacing the ugly carpet with a new orange shag might not be the best idea, but a beige Berber-style carpet could be just the thing.

## Retail Value

Retail value is the value assigned to a given improvement for sale to the public. While retail value is a common measurement of value, it is not always a good one. Paying retail value for a home improvement could cause you to lose a percentage of your investment. The other problem with looking at the retail value of a home improvement is the wide variances in what the retail value actually is. For example, one contractor may quote a price of $2,000 to build your new deck, while another contractor may offer the same deck at a price of $1,500. At first glance the lower price seems to be the better value, but that is not always the case.

Home improvements are seldom like name-brand items in a store. Shopping for the best deal on a specific brand and model of a kitchen appliance is easy. You know you are comparing identical products at various retail outlets, and you can determine where the best deal is with minimal knowledge of the appliance.

Home improvements are not as easy to compare. One contractor's deck is not likely to be identical to the next contractor's. The differences in materials and workmanship can vary a great deal. This makes choosing the right improvement and the right contractors much harder than finding the best price on a refrigerator.

To complicate matters further, geographic locations can play a significant role in the value of any home improvement. Let's say you want to build a garage and none of the other homes in your neighborhood has a garage. Is building a garage on your property a good idea? Probably not. Having the only home in the area with a garage could be a good selling feature, but the improvement probably is not cost effective. However, if you were the only house in the neighborhood that did *not* have a garage, adding one could do wonders for both the salability and the value of your home.

Most consumers never consider resale value when purchasing home improvement services. This is unfortunate. Most people will sell their homes at some point, often within less than ten years of making a major home improvement. When homeowners don't think about the resale value of their investments in the beginning, they are often disappointed in the end. Retail value alone is not enough when assessing the value of home improvements.

## Market Value

Market value is the value assigned to a property that is being marketed for sale. As it relates to home improvements, market value can be dramatically different from retail value. A swimming pool with an original retail value of $20,000 may have a market value of only $10,000. The extreme difference between these two values can come as quite a shock to the uninformed consumer.

Market value is often thought to be the same as appraised value. While this is frequently the case, there are exceptions. Professional appraisals of real estate are estimates. They are usually very accurate estimates, but there are market conditions that can prove market values to be less than appraised values.

The market value is the price the market is willing to pay. While your $20,000 pool may be worth $10,000 on an appraisal report, the buying public may not be willing to pay anything extra for it. In fact, to some buyers, the swimming pool may be considered a liability and thereby reduce your home's market value to that segment of the market.

## Appraised Value

The appraised value of a property is considered to be the most reliable estimate of value. Banks, brokers, buyers, and sellers all rely on appraised values for most real estate transactions. While appraisals are not infallible, they are typically the best measure of cash value for real estate and home improvements.

## Sales Enhancement Value

Translating sales enhancement value into dollars and cents is difficult. Like personal enjoyment improvements, sales enhancement improvements have a type of value that is not easily identified. These improvements are made to help sell a property. Some home sellers will be willing to lose a portion of their home improvement investment if the loss results in a timely sale of their home. For anyone in a have-to-sell situation, these improvements can be of great value. On the other hand, for people not under pressure to sell their property, the value of an improvement for sales motivation can be very low.

## Cost Approach

The cost approach is one of the methods appraisers use in determining a value for real estate. For appraisers and contractors, this approach is fairly easy. It involves nothing more than estimating the cost to construct a home, a building, or an improvement. The cost approach is also relatively easy for homeowners to use in determining home improvement values.

As a homeowner, all you have to do is contact a cross-section of contractors and have them submit quotes for the work you are considering having done. If you get five bids from five different contractors, you can draw some conclusion as to the cost of your proposed improvement. This method is necessary, but you will not usually get enough information to make a wise decision.

When you think about putting value on a home improvement, you should think in terms of *phases*. The first phase is the out-of-pocket expense for the project. The cost approach is the best way to determine your acquisition cost for the proposed work.

There are four basic ways that you, the homeowner, can go about finding a fair price or value for the work you have planned. All of the methods discussed in this section are based on the assumption that you will not take an active part in the work. We will look at how your evaluation might differ as a do-it-yourselfer or general contractor a little later.

### APPRAISER

Perhaps the easiest and most reliable way to arrive at a value for work is to hire an independent appraiser. If you give an appraisal firm the plans and specifications for the work you wish to have done, the firm can provide you with a before-and-after appraisal. The appraisal report will indicate the present value of your home and the anticipated value of the home once the improvements are made.

This type of research can get expensive, but for large improvements the expense is worthwhile. Don't be surprised if the appraisal fees are around $500. While this method is not cheap, it is safe and unbiased. This type of report will show you a value for your project, but don't rely on the value to be the same as the price of the work.

### CONTRACTORS

Having contractors quote prices for the work is a fine way to establish cost, but it does not necessarily represent value. Ideally, you should deal with contractors to establish cost and with appraisers to establish value. Of course, some improvements cost less than the fees for professional appraisers. You must use common sense in deciding how far to carry your research. If all you want to do is replace your front door, it would be ludicrous to call in professional appraisers. On the other hand, if you will be investing $15,000 in an attic conversion, the cost of a certified appraisal would be money well spent.

When you talk with contractors, it is critical that you provide all the contractors with detailed plans and specifications for the work you want done. Don't leave any variables in your plans, and don't allow the contractors to substitute brands of materials. One contractor might bid the job with a toilet that costs $125, while the next remodeler's bid includes a toilet that sells for $50. If you cannot compare apples to apples, your cost estimates will prove disappointing.

### COST ESTIMATING MANUALS

If you have a basic understanding of the work that will be done for you, it is possible to use cost estimating manuals to arrive at estimated prices for the work. These manuals can produce estimates that are remarkably accurate. However, they can also give numbers that are not in line with your local conditions.

These pricing manuals are published by various companies, and all of the books are based on averages. There are special multipliers that allow you to refine the generic information for your geographical region, but even so, be careful; real-world prices are often more or less than these helpful books can predict.

Many of the cost figures in the estimating books I have used are inflated. As a general contractor, remodeler, plumbing contractor, and real estate broker, I have been exposed to a lot of real-world pricing and value. I currently live in Maine, but much of my experience was gained in Virginia. In addition to these two states, I have worked in many other parts of the country, and I have seldom seen residential jobs cost as much as some of the estimating books say they should. I know many contractors use these pricing books to establish retail prices, so the books can give you a hint of what to expect. However, don't put all of your trust in generic numbers. You will have to research your local market for precise pricing and value information.

PRICE SHOPPING

Price shopping is another way for you to develop a guesstimate of what your improvement costs will be. If you know what materials will be used in your job, you can call or visit local suppliers to get pricing information.

Once you know the cost of the materials, you could double the figure to come up with a ballpark price for your jobs. Many contractors use this method to establish their selling prices. While this method is not very scientific, it is frequently accurate enough to suffice.

## Square-Footage Pricing

Square-footage pricing is often used to calculate the cost of large jobs, such as major room additions, attic conversions, and the construction of new homes. This method is used by appraisers, builders, remodelers, and cost-estimating books.

While the square-footage method is a quick way to arrive at a working figure, it is not always accurate. Many factors can skew the effectiveness of this method. If you are dealing with new homes, all of similar size and quality, the square-footage method is pretty accurate. It is also effective in pricing decks and porches, but it can go haywire when used to figure an attic conversion or addition.

If you were to build two additions containing the same square footage, you might think both additions would cost the same. They might if all the elements were the same, but what if one of the additions was a family room and the other was a master bedroom suite with a full bath. The plumbing in the second addition would cause the price to go up several thousand dollars. You must be careful if you choose to use a square-footage approach for esti-

mating costs.

## Comparable-Sales Approach

When you are concerned with the resale value of an improvement, you should use a comparable-sales approach in establishing value. This is the method depended upon most often by residential real estate appraisers.

Remember earlier when we talked about building a garage when your home was the only home in the neighborhood without a garage? Well, in a way, we were talking about making a decision based on a comparable-sales approach. Since the house without the garage was unique in the neighborhood, its value would probably suffer from the lack of a garage.

Appraisers try to work with at least three comparable sales when appraising a property. They look for similar properties that have sold as recently as possible, and hopefully no more than six months ago. Using detailed data sheets, the appraisers list all the important features of the properties. Then a comparison is made of each property sold. This allows the appraiser to define an anticipated market value for a given feature, for example, a garage.

Let me give you a simple example of how this works. Let's say you want to add a standard two-car garage to your home. You hire an appraiser to perform a before-and-after appraisal of your property, with and without the garage. For the sake of our example, assume four houses of similar style and age to yours have sold within your neighborhood in the last ninety days. Two of the houses had standard two-car garages and two of them did not have garages.

In this example, the appraiser's job will be easy. By looking at the price differences between the closed sales, the appraiser can quickly assess the value of a two-car garage. If both of the houses with garages sold for about $8,000 more than the two houses without garages, and all other features were about the same, the market value of the garage is about $8,000.

In reality, performing a comparable-sales evaluation is rarely so simple, but the example does show clearly the principle behind such a study. This method of evaluation is preferred by banks, builders, brokers, and appraisers for residential properties.

### Do-It-Yourself Equity

Do-it-yourself equity is a wonderful asset. You invest some time in fixing up your home, and all of a sudden, you have more equity in the property—if the job is done well. It is possible to build substantial sums of equity through the right home improvements. The equity can be used as leverage for borrowing power, or it can be left alone until the house is sold and a handsome profit is recognized.

There are two ways to build do-it-yourself equity. You can choose an improvement and do all the work yourself, or you can act as a general contractor. Either way, you stand to build equity in your home.

By doing the work yourself, you could build equity equal to about one-half the retail value of the improvement. For example, if you build a deck that has a retail value of $2,000, you might only spend $1,000 in materials. When the job is done, the time you have spent on the project translates into an equity gain of $1,000. Of course, the numbers don't always work this way; sometimes they are better, and sometimes they are not as good.

By acting as your own general contractor, you can save up to 30 percent of the total retail job cost. Most jobs will allow you to save around 20 percent, and big jobs might only offer savings of 10 percent. Small jobs are usually loaded with a higher percentage of income for a general contractor, and those jobs are the ones that can yield a savings of 30 per-cent or more.

If you are improving your home to build equity, you want to choose your projects carefully. For example, it is conceivable that you would spend the same amount of money to finish your basement into living quarters as you might spend to convert your attic to habitable space. If this were the case, you would almost always be better off to convert your attic. When it comes to value, living space in an attic is usually worth considerably more than living space in a basement. You might spend the same amount of money, but you will gain much more equity with the smarter of the two improvements.

## PUTTING THE PIECES TOGETHER

Assessing the value of your home improvements will require putting the pieces together from various evaluation methods. Pegging the right price and value takes some effort on your part, but the reward is well worth it. Rather than spending your hard-earned money on an improvement that is a flop as an investment, you will be able to make wise buying decisions.

Now that you have an overview of the various methods used to predict prices and values, let's move on to our first type of improvement for financial considerations. Chapter Two addresses the issue of landscaping.

# LANDSCAPING 2

Landscaping is a key element in the appearance and value of a home. It is hard to find a book or chart that deals with home values and home improvements that doesn't include landscaping. Finding landscaping placed in the top-five favorite categories for home improvements is not unusual. As it relates to value, landscaping often finds its way into the list of top-ten projects to do. However, when a return on your investment is important, you must be cautious not to become too extravagant in your landscaping plans.

The term "landscaping" can cover a broad range of improvements. It can be applied to sodding, seeding, shrubbery, trees, gravel, fish ponds, latticework, flowers, and so on. A landscaping project can cost less than $25 or more than $2,500. Homeowners can do a majority of their own landscaping tasks, but a host of professionals can be found to help with everything from design to installation.

Landscaping is big business, and it can cost big bucks. Is landscaping a wise investment? Yes, in moderation, but you must know when enough is enough. Too much landscaping will not show up well on an appraisal report.

How important is landscaping to a home's value? It can be very important. A home with no landscaping is barren, often unattractive, and unlikely to present strong curb appeal to prospective buyers. At the very least, most homes should be adorned with foundation shrubbery.

Can you recover the money you invest in modest landscaping? Yes, in most cases you can, if you keep your investment at a moderate level. Some ap-praisers believe you can recover the full investment of foundation shrubbery and minor landscaping. However, some surveys indicate you won't recover more than 60 percent of major landscaping investments. The key to recovering your cost is moderate landscaping that conforms to local customs.

Are there times landscaping is not a good idea? It's not so much that there are times landscaping is wrong, but there are situations in which the wrong type of landscaping can have a negative impact on a property. For example, planting tall, bushy decorations around your house could make some buyers nervous. They may fear the tall greenery will provide a place for burglars to hide. The installation of a garden pond may alienate some people. If they have small children, they may be concerned about the risk of drowning.

Even though you may not be considering the possibility of selling your house, you should keep resale values and results in mind. When an appraiser is estimating the value of your improvement, market appeal and demand will be factors in the value assigned.

Let's take an in-depth look at some landscaping projects and see how they rate in the battle of cost versus value.

## TREES

Trees can certainly be a part of your landscaping plans, but trees can be both large and expensive. Installing trees by yourself may not be practical or possible. Large trees can easily cost hundreds of dollars. Even small trees will run between $50 and $100.

Should you plant trees in your lawn? This is a tough question to answer without knowing what the surrounding properties are like. Normally, it is safe to plant small flowering trees in any lawn. However, arranging the installation of large, leafy trees will not only be expensive, it can provide future problems. As the trees get larger, falling limbs could damage your home and leaf maintenance might become an unwanted chore.

Before investing too much money in large trees, weigh all your options and responsibilities. If you decide to have big trees planted, do your homework before spending your money. Consult with experts, possibly at your local nursery, for the types of trees best suited to your location. It is wise to have soil samples taken prior to investing in expensive plantings. The soil may not be suitable for some types of trees.

If you decide to tackle this project on your own, obtain information for the proper installation and care of your new improvements.

In general, trees are expensive and do not provide the best return on your landscaping dollar. Stick with small, manageable trees, and keep your costs down. If you spend thousands of dollars on trees, you may find that money not only does not grow on trees, it is hard to recover from them.

## SHRUBS

Shrubs, in limited quantities, are a good investment. This type of landscaping can be done by any handy homeowner, and the per-unit cost is very reasonable. It is possible to buy foundation shrubs for less than $10 apiece, and you should recover all of your investment. Your home will be more attractive, you will spend a small amount of money for the benefits of the shrubs, and if you decide to sell your home, you should get most, if not all, of your investment back.

The installation of eight foundation shrubs, even at $25 apiece, will only cost $200. The total cost of the job could be more if you elect to install edging, mulching, or similar dressings, but in any event, the improvement will have a minimal cost and a major impact.

As a builder, I have installed foundation shrubs on all the houses I've built on speculation. As a broker, I've seen the reactions from prospective buyers when the foundation of a home was "naked." I can tell you from both of these positions, foundation shrubbery is appreciated by the public and by prospective buyers.

While this is not a how-to-do-it book, there is something you should know about the installation of foundation shrubbery. When you plant it, don't place it too close to the foundation. Allow room for the plants to grow without crowding each other or the foundation. Many types of plants can cause mildew and moisture problems for a house if they are planted too close to the foundation.

How far from the foundation should the plants be planted? The distance for clearance will vary with the different types of plants. Three feet should be an adequate distance for most types of foundation shrubs, but keep in mind the mature size of the plant you choose. Your local nursery can advise you on this.

## SEEDING

Seeding is not a common improvement for existing homes, but there are times it is necessary even for established lawns. When the grounds around your home develop brown or bare spots, it's time to take action. Keeping a healthy green lawn around your home does much for its appearance and value.

Seeding is not a complicated job. With a bag of seed, a few hand tools, and a rented roller, you should be able to handle the job on your own. It is important to talk with experts to determine the proper preparation for seeding. Different types of grass have different needs.

If you have a small lawn, you should be able to seed it for less than $150. However, if you need to arrange for the delivery and spreading of topsoil, expect some steep fees. As an old friend once told me, "Some things in life are dirt cheap, but dirt isn't one of them."

Unfortunately, the cost of repairing and maintaining your lawn is unlikely to be recovered if you sell your house. Homes are expected to have satisfactory grounds, and this improvement falls into the maintenance category.

## SODDING

Sodding is a quick fix for ailing lawns, but it is not an inexpensive proposition. Sod is expensive, and unless it is installed and cared for properly, it is likely to die. Sod is also very heavy and can be difficult to work with.

Fresh sod should be installed the same day it is delivered to the job site. Getting the rolls of grass and dirt into place and seated into the prepared soil is not an easy job. If you decide to tackle this task on your own, be prepared for a long day and a sore back.

The cost of sodding is much more than that of seeding: at least double and possibly quite a bit more. If you are only repairing a few damaged sections of lawn, sod is the best option. If, however, you are reworking the entire grounds, seeding is more economical, if you have the patience to wait for it to grow. As far as a return on your investment, sod falls into the same maintenance category as seeding.

## FLOWERS

Flowers have the power to change the complexion of a home. Planting colorful blossoms in flower boxes, beds, and baskets can do much for the curb appeal of your home. The cost for flowers is minimal, but the visual impact is enormous.

You are not likely to see any equity gain in your home from planting flowers, but coming home will be a greater pleasure, and your neighbors will appreciate the fresh look.

## FENCING

Fencing can be an attractive addition to your property, but don't expect it to increase your equity or resale value by much. It is possible for decorative fencing to help sell a house, and fences can provide varying degrees of personal enjoyment, but they are generally not considered a great investment for your home-improvement money.

The appraiser I consulted for this book told me that it is difficult to allow much value for the average fence on most appraisals. Unless all the houses around you have fenced yards, you should think long and hard before installing fencing. Of course, if you want the fence to contain your children or pets, there is nothing wrong with acting on the personal enjoyment angle of the improvement. You should be aware, however, that the monetary value of the fencing will probably be much less than what you invest in it. Let's take a look at the most popular types of fencing.

### Board Fencing

Board fencing can be made up on the job site, or it can be purchased in prefabricated panels. This type of fencing requires routine maintenance, in the form of painting or staining, and the maintenance can be a negative factor in the fence's value.

Make no mistake about it, a good quality board fence is not cheap. To do the job right, you will have to dig or auger holes and pour a foundation for each post. If you don't install the proper footing for the posts, the fence can shift and raise when the ground freezes.

Even working with prefabricated panels, the proper installation of an extensive fencing system is best left to professionals, and professional installation adds considerably to an already expensive project.

As for cost, the materials, depending on what exactly is used, will run about $10 per linear foot. To fence a building lot with dimensions of 100' X 100' with a fence about 4 feet high could easily cost $4,000 in materials alone. Add professional labor fees, and your fencing job could cost around $8,000. This is a lot of money to invest for a personal-enjoyment improvement.

### Others

There are, of course, other types of fencing. Split-rail fencing is a favorite for marking property boundaries and driveway entrances. Chain link fence is still used in many locations, but it is not as well received by the public as an attractive wood fence. Stockade or palisade fencing is often used to provide privacy in the backyards of townhouses. There are plenty of types of fencing to choose from, but all of it is expensive, and none of it is likely to pay for itself on an appraisal report.

## PATIOS

Patios may be stretching the description of landscaping, but since they are installed on the ground and don't necessarily attach to the home, we will cover them in this section.

Typically, patios don't add much value to a property. They can make a home more appealing and more usable, but don't count on much of an equity gain or a high resale value.

There are numerous materials available for patio construction. Since there are so many ways to build a patio and such a variety of choices in materials, let's look at a few of the most popular ones.

### Brick Patios

Brick patios are common. The bricks can be set in sand or mortar, and the results can be quite attractive. Designs can be made in these patios with creative placement of the bricks, and you don't have to be an accomplished brick mason to make a handsome patio.

Setting the bricks in sand offers many advantages to the do-it-yourselfer. Mistakes are easier to correct in sand than when the bricks are laid in mortar, and no special skill is needed in getting mortar mixed properly.

Preparing the base for the patio is a pivotal point in a successful installation. Once the base is ready, patience is the key ingredient to a professional-looking job. Material costs vary from place to place, but all the materials needed for a brick patio set in sand should cost less than $5 per square foot, even for patios with under 100 square feet. This is one job when the old rule of doubling the cost of materials to arrive at the retail price of a professional job is not likely to be accurate. To be safe, you should figure on a total professional cost for this type of job to run between $12 and $15 per square foot. If you opt to make your brick patio with a mortar base, the cost will be about the same or slightly higher.

### Concrete Patios

Concrete patios are one way to get a low-cost patio that will provide years of dependable service. They are not as stylish as some of the other types of patios, but they have been used for years and are still acceptable.

Handy homeowners can manage the installation of small concrete patios, but it is important to do the job right. Without the proper preparation of excavating, wire mesh, expansion joints, and so forth, the concrete will crack. Perhaps the most challenging aspect of a concrete patio is finishing the concrete. Many people use a broom to produce a brushed finish. This requires less skill than a floated finish, and the patio is not as slippery when wet.

The materials for this type of job should cost in the neighborhood of $1.75 per square foot. In this case, doubling the cost of materials will give you a reasonable guesstimate for professional installations. Even though this type of patio is very affordable, it is questionable as to how valuable the project is for equity building or resale.

As a variation of the standard concrete patio, some contractors mix small decorative gravel into the top of the concrete. The gravel adds texture to the patio for safety and makes the surface more appealing to the eye.

### Other Types

Other types of patios are made from slate, flagstone, and patio blocks. These types of patios can be set in sand or mortar. Costs for this type of patio material can range from about $3.50 per square foot to over $6.00 per square foot. Labor rates for professionals are similar to those encountered with brick patios. To be safe, triple the estimated cost of your materials to arrive at a total retail price from professional contractors. In other words, if the materials for your job will cost $5.00 per square foot, don't be surprised if professionals quote a labor-and-materials price of $15 per square foot.

## WALKWAYS

Walkways (Figures 2-1 and 2-2) are very similar to patios, both in the methods of installation and in their value. However, walkways generally command a higher value on an appraisal than patios do. Don't expect a huge increase in your home's equity when adding a walkway, but if you don't have one, you should consider this project. People prefer houses with walkways, and while appraisers may not give you much for the walkway you install, they may deduct value from your house for not having one.

The cost of building a walkway is very similar to the cost of constructing a patio, in terms of square-footage pricing. If you have a limited amount of money and are undecided between spending it on a walkway or a patio, go with the walkway.

## GARDEN PONDS

Not everyone appreciates an ornamental garden pond. I like them and have built this type of relaxing water garden for myself in the past. As I mentioned earlier, some people will see the pond as a safety hazard for their children. Others will see it as a breeding ground for mosquitoes. And then there will be people who are enthralled with the beauty and peace associated with the private pond.

Decorative ponds don't have to be expensive to build, but they can be. As far as appraisals go, you won't like the rate of return for a garden pond. This improvement definitely falls into the personal-enjoyment category.

The cost of materials for a simple in-ground pond, lined with a plastic liner and controlled by na-ture, is less than $500. If you set the pond up with a pump and filter, the cost for materials can rise dramatically. The cost for a pump, filter, liner, and minimal pond-side landscaping can quickly exceed $1,500. Bringing in professionals to install this enchanting pool could more than double the cost.

After the pond construction is complete, there will be the cost of aquatic plants and fish. Depending upon your tastes, this can add hundreds of dollars to the finished cost. Unless you are installing the pond for your own enjoyment and peace of mind, this is not the remodeling project for you.

This brings us to the end of landscaping. There are, of course, many other ways to spruce up the grounds around your home, but this chapter has covered the projects most often questioned.

Now we are ready to move on to Chapter Three and explore the options and values of outside recreational improvements. If you are contemplating installation of a swimming pool or a tennis court, you should read the next chapter before you get out your checkbook.

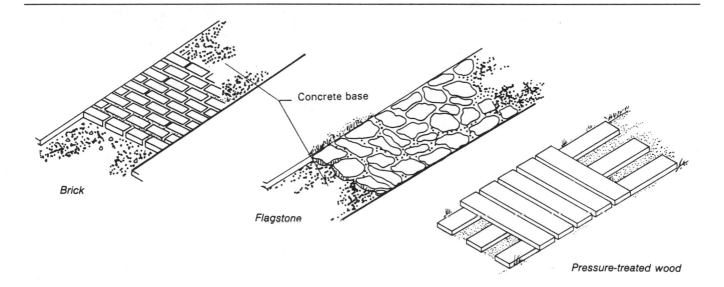

Brick

Concrete base

Flagstone

Pressure-treated wood

Figure 2-1. *Examples of brick, flagstone, and wood walkway styles. Courtesy of U.S. Dept. of Agriculture.*

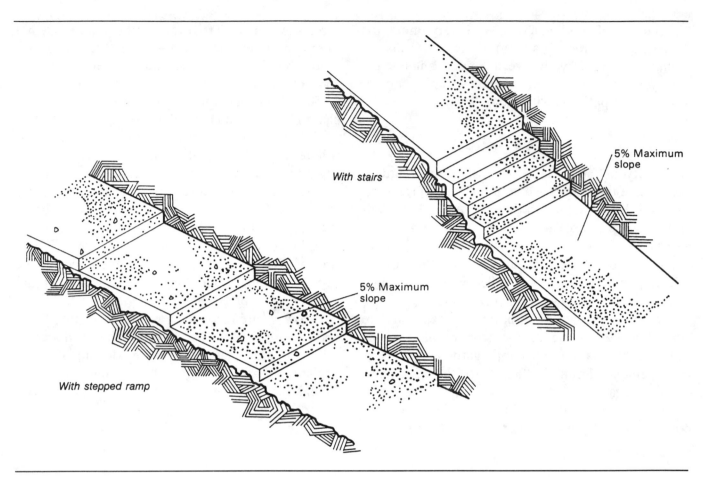

5% Maximum slope

With stairs

5% Maximum slope

With stepped ramp

Figure 2-2. *Examples of walkways built on sloping ground. Courtesy of U.S. Dept. of Agriculture.*

# OUTSIDE RECREATIONAL IMPROVEMENTS 3

This is not a long chapter, but if you are thinking about investing in an outside recreational improvement for your home, it is written just for you. What is an outside recreational improvement? One of the most common forms of outside recreational improvements is a swimming pool. Both above-ground and in-ground pools are discussed in this chapter, and you might not like hearing the truth about the resale value of these items. What else could be considered an outside recreational improvement? A tennis court would fall into this category, and gazebos and spas could fit the description. Even elaborate playgrounds could fit the mold.

Do people really invest major amounts of money in these types of home improvements? You bet they do, and many of them are devastated when they discover the effects the improvements have on the resale value of their properties. I'm sure you are already getting the idea that these playful projects don't provide strong returns to their investors, and you are right. This group of improvements is definitely in the personal-enjoyment category. To see just how much the price for pleasure is, let's look at some specific examples.

## ABOVE-GROUND SWIMMING POOLS

Above-ground swimming pools have come a long way since my days in the wading pool out back. Today's above-ground pools are sophisticated and can be very large. The attraction to this type of pool is its lower cost over that of a conventional in-ground pool, the lack of serious excavation work, and the mobility of the unit.

Are above-ground pools good investments? Not likely. They are fine if you are buying them for enjoyment only, but if you are expecting to get your money back out of the investment, forget it.

How much does an above-ground pool cost? Well, that depends on the size and the quality, but I can give you an example. A family-size pool with the necessary filtering system and accessories can be bought for less than $3,500. This is your basic department-store variety, and it is the type most often purchased. You could spend a good deal more for a pool of similar size, but this one will do for the purpose of our illustration.

You buy the pool and related equipment for about $3,500. Then you get to erect it. If you think putting a bicycle together is a hair-pulling experience, wait until you try to set up your new pool. After days of frustration, my guess is that you will call in a professional installer. Boom! The price shoots up.

Okay, you have the pool standing and all the parts hooked up. Now you need about 15,000 gallons of water. I don't think you want to try pumping 15,000 gallons of water into your pool with a garden hose. So what will you do? You will probably call a company that brings a tanker truck to your home and fills the pool. Uh oh, the price just went up some more.

If you want a heater, cover, or other handy accessories to make using the pool more enjoyable, you are going to have to reach back into your pocket. The cost just seems to keep escalating.

All in all, by the time you are done, you probably have between $5,000 and $7,500 invested in your new yard toy. With what you've gone through to install the pool, it is unlikely you will have any desire to move it if you sell your house. Oh, and did the pool salesperson tell you about the local ordinance that requires all swimming pools to be enclosed with fencing? Don't worry, the local code enforcement officer will tell you.

Not all areas require pools to be fenced, but most do, and you've already seen what the cost and rate of return for fencing are. It is quite conceivable that your final investment in the pool and related necessities will top off somewhere near $10,000.

Now, how much does this capital investment amount to on the new appraised value of your home? It depends on many circumstances, but it would be surprising if the value on the appraisal report exceeded 30 percent of your investment. Some experts claim in-ground pools only return between 20 and 50 percent of their original cost, and you can bet that an above-ground pool won't do that well.

## IN-GROUND SWIMMING POOLS

In-ground swimming pools (Figure 3-1) produce similar results to above-ground pools, but the money involved is much greater. Depending on the site conditions and size of the in-ground pool installed, you could pay up to $30,000 for the improvement. With hard bargaining and some compromises, you might get by with an out-of-pocket expense of $20,000. If you will agree that an average investment in an in-ground pool is $25,000 (and this figure is considered low by many standards), you stand to lose at least $12,500 when you sell your home.

Let's say you have the pool installed and use it for five years before selling your house. You will be paying approximately $2,500 per year, not counting maintenance expenses, for the privilege of swimming in your private pool. If this fits into your budget and desires, fine, but don't say I didn't warn you of the poor payoff on the pool when you sell the house.

Some statistics indicate that pools return only 20 percent of their initial investment. If this is the case, your annual cost has been $4,000. According to the licensed appraiser I talked with, a pool could return anywhere from 0 percent to 50 percent of its original cost.

If pools are such poor investments, why do so many people have them installed? Some people have no idea what their personal swimming pleasure is going to cost them in the long run. Others are aware of what they are doing, but are willing to pay the price for what they want. As long as you are aware of the potential shortfall of your investment, buying a swimming pool can be a lot of fun.

## TENNIS COURTS

Tennis courts are not as common at most residences as swimming pools, but they fall into the same category of personal-enjoyment improvements that are very unlikely to pay for themselves. The cost of a quality court hinges on many factors: site condition, type of construction, quality of construction, and so on. But a good court can deflate your bank account by at least $20,000 and a cost of $30,000 wouldn't be unheard of. Again, as long as you are willing to pay to play, investing in a tennis court is fine, but don't expect much return on your investment.

## GAZEBOS

Gazebos are not going to lose as much of their initial value as swimming pools or tennis courts, but they are still not considered great investments.

The size of the gazebo constructed is an important factor in the cost of this improvement. The amount of labor you provide personally will also affect the final cost of your project. Gazebos usually have many angles and require fairly sophisticated carpentry skills. It can be very difficult for the average homeowner to build a good-looking gazebo.

Another major factor in the cost of a gazebo is the types of materials used for construction. If you choose asphalt shingles to roof your gazebo, the cost will be much less than if you decide to use cedar shakes as a roofing material. The difference in this type of cost will not be as noticeable in a small structure as it would be for a larger building.

What type of foundation will the gazebo have?

If the structure is built on a pier foundation, the cost of construction will be more than if it is built on wooden skids. There are many options in materials that can affect the cost of any gazebo.

If you figure a cost of $10 per square foot for materials, you should be in the ballpark. Due to the many angles and sometimes complicated methods of construction, professional labor rates can run up to $30 per square foot, giving a total cost for labor and materials of $40 a square foot. Of course, you might find a carpenter who will build the structure for you at a labor rate of $15 per square foot.

If we say an average total cost for construction is $35 per square foot, a small gazebo, say one with 100 square feet, is going to set you back about $3,500. The cost per square foot should go down as the size of the structure increases.

So what is a gazebo that costs $3,500 worth? Well, that depends on whom you ask. If you agree to pay $3,500 for the improvement, it must be worth $3,500 to you. To an appraiser, the value might range from $2,000 to $3,500. However, a gazebo is not considered living space, and therefore, it generally suffers on an appraisal report.

If the gazebo is kept to a moderate size and is built from good but not elaborate materials, it will probably return at least half of its cost.

## OUTDOOR SPAS

Outdoor spas are more popular in some areas of the country than others. Having a bubbling whirlpool countersunk into your deck may be well worthwhile in selected neighborhoods, but putting the spa outside reduces your chances for recovering its value.

Self-contained spas can be purchased for less than $2,000. There are, of course, models that cost several thousand dollars more. For the sake of our example, let's assume the retail value of the spa is $2,500.

The types of spas we are talking about here do not require plumbing connections, and they are mobile units. They can be placed on a deck or patio, in a gazebo, or in the middle of your family room. Since the units are able to be moved, they can be taken with you if you ever sell your home; this gives them an advantage over most home improvements.

Unless the spa is permanently installed in a way that would make its removal difficult or impossible, the tub will be considered personal property. Normally, appraisers don't base a home's value on personal property, such as window treatments, wood stoves, and in this case, spas. Therefore, adding a spa to your home may not increase the home's value at all on an appraisal report.

If you decide to sell the spa, you are unlikely to recover more than 50 percent of its original cost. You should look at the purchase of an outdoor spa as a personal-enjoyment improvement. It can add charm to your property, and it can increase your home's value, but don't expect the improvement to pay for itself.

## PLAYGROUNDS

If you have children and a private yard, you may consider constructing a playground. This type of improvement can only be looked at as a personal-enjoyment improvement.

The materials for a playground can cost well over $1,000. You can buy kits to construct elaborate playgrounds, and you can buy normal building materials to build the play area. There are also sets, both wood and metal, available from various retail stores.

If you build much of a playground, you will invest at least $500. This is not a lot of money by today's standards, and if your children enjoy the improvement for a few years, it is probably money well spent. However, from an appraisal point of view, the improvement is normally worthless. If anything, it may lower your home's value. The playground will undoubtedly take up space in the yard, and the grounds in and around the play area will most likely be worn down to bare earth. The cost of returning the area to a natural lawn could be significant, and an appraiser may lower the overall value of your home to reflect this cost.

Well, we have completed our list of outside recreational improvements, and we are about to move on to exterior home improvements. The improvements in the next chapter are more traditional and will apply to many more people than the recreational improvements in this chapter might.

Figure 3-1. *In-ground swimming pool. Courtesy of Velux-America, Inc.*

# EXTERIOR HOME IMPROVEMENTS 4

Exterior home improvements are often either ignored or done in haste, without much research. It is easy to be talked into having vinyl siding installed on your home, but is the maintenance-free siding (as it is so often called) really a good investment? For that matter, is vinyl siding truly maintenance free? Would a new coat of paint be a more viable alternative to exterior walls requiring attention? This question and many others like it are addressed in this chapter.

The improvements you make to the exterior of your home are subject to weather and to public opinion. If you allow your teenager to paint a bedroom purple, not many people are going to see the bold decorating statement. However, if you were to paint the siding of your home purple, the color would be out there for all the world to see and judge. Exterior improvements should not be made in haste, and they should not be taken lightly.

## HOME-IMPROVEMENT SALESPEOPLE

Home-improvement salespeople often find themselves in the news, and generally, it is not for winning sales awards. Newspapers all across the country carry stories of how slick salespeople have either sold their services at highly inflated prices or defrauded customers. This type of news scares the public and brings legitimate home-improvement contractors under intense scrutiny.

Many people are susceptible to unscrupulous salespeople. It is easy for a sales professional to con-

vince an average homeowner that a particular home improvement is needed. It is also easy for these salespeople to sell a percentage of their jobs right on the spot. Homeowners become concerned about their homes and act to have problems corrected or improvements made without doing the research that they should. It is not really the homeowner's fault; he frequently doesn't know the right questions to ask, and he has no idea what it should cost to have a particular improvement done. This trusting homeowner gets a hard-ball sales pitch, an offer of easy, on-the-spot financing, and before he knows it, he has signed a contract for the repairs or improvements.

This type of activity goes on all the time, and many people never realize they have paid too much for the services or products they received. Even if the home-improvement company does a good job and is guilty only of charging above-average prices, the consumer can be hurt financially.

While this book isn't going to show you how to choose a reputable contractor, it is going to help you to protect yourself from outrageous prices. By using this book as one of the pieces of your home-improvement puzzle, you can work to ensure a good job at a fair price. Let's look at some of the types of exterior home improvements you might be considering and assess their costs and values.

## PAINTING

Painting is a very common exterior home improvement. Some people paint their homes to change the color, but most homeowners paint their houses to maintain its value and physical condition. When you are establishing the value of an intended improvement, you have to investigate all angles of the job.

Is there a difference between painting your home to change its color and painting it to maintain its physical condition? Yes; painting only to change colors is a desire, and painting to maintain the quality of your home is a necessity. This difference can have an effect on how the value of the improvement is assessed. Since the two approaches should be evaluated differently, let's look first at the value of painting out of desire.

## Painting by Preference

Painting by preference must be considered a personal-enjoyment improvement. The job is not being done as needed maintenance, and it will not, under most conditions, increase the value of a home. Frame houses are expected to be painted and in good repair. The fact that you replaced gray paint that was a year old with beige paint isn't likely to influence the appraised value of your home.

How much will it cost to paint your home? The cost depends on many factors. These factors might include the condition of the siding, the quality of the paint used, the size of your home, the style of your home, and the accessibility to areas requiring paint.

If you decide to paint the house yourself, the cost of materials is not difficult to estimate, assuming the siding is in good condition. The labels on paint containers indicate how much coverage you can expect to get out of a given quantity of paint. For example, a one-gallon can of exterior paint might be rated to cover 400 square feet of surface area.

Some simple math will tell you approximately how much paint you will need. Let's assume you have a ranch-style home with dimensions of 24' X 44'. We will further assume that the exterior walls have a vertical exposure of 9 feet. To figure out your paint needs, let's start with the front of the house.

The front of the house is 44 feet wide and 9 feet high. That gives you a total square footage (44 X 9) of 396 square feet. Of course, there are windows and a door that consume a portion of this square footage, but don't worry about those items right now.

The back wall has the same dimensions as the front wall, so you also have 396 square feet of surface area on the back wall. Adding the totals of the front and back, you have 792 square feet.

The end walls are a little more difficult to figure. Assuming the house has a standard gable roof, the gable ends of the house must be accounted for. The ends are 24 feet wide. To start with, we will multiply the 24 feet by the 9 feet of full-width vertical wall. When we do this, we come up with a figure of 216 square feet. If we add the totals of the two ends, we have 432 square feet, not counting the gables.

The gables at their lowest points have a width of 24 feet, but the width is reduced as the wall rises to the peak of the roof. You could measure the dimensions of the triangle formed with the gable and work out the square footage, or you can make an estimated guess while keeping your feet on the ground.

If the height of the gable is 12 feet and the width is as described, you could multiply the height by half of the width for a reasonable estimate of the square footage. In doing so, you would come up with a number of 120 square feet. For the purposes of rough estimating, this is close enough. Adding the two gable ends together, you would have 240 square feet.

The total square footage for all the walls is 1,464 square feet (792+432+240). If we know each gallon of paint is rated to cover 400 square feet, we can divide 1,464 by 400 and see that we will need about four gallons of paint per coat.

Now, what about the windows and doors? You could eliminate the square footage they consume from your estimate, but you should allow for waste in your estimating. By ignoring the windows and doors in estimating the amount of paint needed for your siding, you should arrive at a number that will not cause you to run out of paint. You will also have to figure on some paint for the trim around the windows, doors, and soffit. A rule-of-thumb guesstimate for this part of the job is two gallons of paint for each coat of paint being applied to the house.

Without getting too technical in how to estimate the paint needed for your house, we will keep this example simple by saying that you are going to apply two coats of paint to the siding. This job is estimated to require eight gallons of paint. If we assume the paint costs $20 per gallon, your total paint cost for the siding will be $160. The paint cost for the trim will add another $80 to your total.

Since you are probably not a professional painter, you may have to rent a ladder and buy brushes, drop cloths, and other miscellaneous items. A fair estimate for a homeowner doing this job could be $300. If the house requires a coat of primer, and many will, the cost might push up to $400.

Your house has 1,056 square feet of living space, so the cost of materials for doing this job will range from $0.28 to $0.38 per square foot of living area. If you hire a professional to paint the home for you, the labor might run between $1,000 and $2,000, with an average of $1,500. Many contractors estimate painting labor at $1.00 per square foot of exterior painted surface area. The house in this example had 1,464 square feet of painted area, so the anticipated cost for labor could be $1,464. It might be more or less, depending on the number and size of doors and windows.

So here is the question, if you spend $1,500 to have your house painted, just to change its color, what will the paint job be worth? Assuming the house was already painted in a conforming color and was in good condition, the $1,500 spent on the improvement will not reflect an increase of the home's value.

## Painting Out of Necessity

Painting out of necessity is a different story. If you have a house with cracked and peeling paint, the disrepair and unappealing look of your home is hurting its value and may be causing the home to deteriorate further. Painting to correct this type of problem makes more sense than painting only to arrive at a new color.

The cost of this job will be higher than the previous example. Since the existing paint is in bad condition, extra labor is required to prepare the painting surface properly. The additional cost of this extra labor will be determined by the amount of work required to get the siding ready to paint. While a good paint job may not increase your home's value, a bad paint job will definitely decrease the property's worth. It makes sense to keep your siding painted and in good repair.

## VINYL SIDING

Let's compare vinyl siding with painted siding. There is a lot of sales hype that indicates vinyl siding is a sensible alternative to painting your home. Is vinyl siding a good investment? Well, let's examine the facts, and then you can decide for yourself.

### Neighborhood Conformity

Neighborhood conformity is one issue that must be addressed in making a decision for or against vinyl siding. If all the houses on your block have stained, natural cedar siding, installing white vinyl siding on your home would be a financial mistake.

Before converting to vinyl siding, look around you. Do the other houses in the area have wood siding or vinyl siding? If there is a dominance of one type or the other, you will normally be better off to run with the pack.

Vinyl siding can be very popular, but it can also be shunned as a sub-par construction material. What controls this swing in perceptions? Local standards have a lot to do with the public perspective of vinyl siding.

There are many subdivisions where every house is covered with vinyl siding. Vinyl siding has been very popular for townhouses and tract housing. It has also been the choice of homeowners seeking reduced exterior maintenance. Even an area's climate can influence the popularity of a particular type of siding.

With so many factors to consider, deciding on the value of vinyl siding is not an easy task. There are some factors that remain static. One of those factors is the conformity factor. If vinyl siding is not common in your area, shy away from it.

### The Maintenance Factor

The maintenance factor of vinyl siding is one of its strongest selling points. The siding is said to be "maintenance free." While it is true that the color is an integral part of the siding and never needs to be replenished with paint, the siding is not always totally maintenance free.

It is common for mildew to collect on vinyl siding in damp areas. When this occurs, the siding must be washed, often by professionals, using power-washing equipment.

If the siding is not installed correctly, the expansion and contraction that is natural in vinyl siding can cause damage to the siding.

As time passes, the color in vinyl siding often fades. The speed with which the fading occurs depends on climatic conditions, but it is likely to occur at some point.

The trim pieces used with vinyl siding are typically flimsy. They can pull loose, break, and cause varying levels of frustration.

So you see, vinyl siding is not always the cure-all to maintenance problems around the exterior of your home.

### The Cost Factor

The cost factor is also an issue in deciding on vinyl versus wood for your siding material. There are many types of siding to from which to choose. When talking about wood siding, pine and cedar are the two most common types. When it comes to vinyl siding, there are numerous designs, colors, and qualities from which to choose.

Prices for siding vary a great deal. Typically, siding is sold in quantities of 100 square feet, referred to as "squares." One square of siding is equal to 100 square feet. If you were to compare the cost of vinyl siding to cedar siding, you would probably find that the vinyl costs less than half as much as the cedar. Typical pricing for vinyl siding ranges from $45 per square to $65 per square. Some types of vinyl with deep wood grains, special colors, and/or beaded edges can run as much as $100 a square.

The cost comparison of vinyl to wood would have to be weighed carefully if you were building a new home, but here we are talking about improving your existing home. Unless you are rehabbing a home that has been neglected for many years, you probably are faced not with a decision of wood siding versus vinyl siding, but a decision of painting versus vinyl siding.

We saw earlier what to expect in the cost of repainting a home. Let's use that same home to see what the cost might be to install vinyl siding.

If you recall, the house in the painting example had a total painting surface of 1,464 square feet. This figure, however, included the windows and doors. Since you would not be installing siding over these areas, let's eliminate the square footage controlled by those openings. For the sake of our example, we will eliminate 264 square feet for windows and doors. This leaves us with 1,200 square feet to cover with siding.

To cover 1,200 square feet of house, we will need twelve squares of siding. At an average cost of $55 per square, this amounts to $660. In addition to the siding, we will need the special trim used when installing the siding. This might run our materials cost up by another $360. While vinyl siding may cost half as much as wood siding, the trim for vinyl can cost three times as much as that used with wood siding. We now have $1,020 in materials. This works out to be about $1.00 for each square foot of habitable space in the home.

There is a good possibility that do-it-yourselfers will need to rent ladders, scaffolding, and a few tools. The rental fees for these items might add another hundred dollars or more to the cost. For the sake of simplicity, we will assume the total cost for a do-it-yourselfer is $1,056, or $1.00 per square foot of living space.

This material take-off does not include the foam insulation boards that should be installed behind the vinyl siding. If the foam backing is not used, the vinyl siding will not lie flat or look good. It will also not have the insulation value of foam-backed vinyl siding. The cost of this backing will probably add another $350 to the price of the job. Now our total list of materials comes to a price of about $1,400, or $1.33 per square foot of living space. Let's compare these material costs with those from the painting example.

In the painting example, the estimated cost for two coats of paint and a coat of primer worked out to be $0.38 per square foot of living area. The cost of materials for the vinyl siding is $1.33 per square foot of living space, or $0.95 per square foot more. So the materials alone for siding this house are about $1,000 more than the cost of paint.

Now, what about labor? An average homeowner can paint a house, but this same homeowner may not possess the skills to install vinyl siding. The job is tricky with new construction, and it can be downright difficult when fitting the siding to an existing house that has sagged and is out of plumb.

If we decide that you will hire professionals to install your new vinyl siding, let's see what the labor might cost. The labor for a professional siding crew will probably run between $1,200 and $1,500 for our sample house. The labor rate for this siding job is very competitive with the labor estimated for painting the house. The difference is that many homeowners can do their own painting but not their own siding installation. Dealing in rough, round numbers, the extra cost for siding the home is about $1,000.

How often will you have to paint your house? The conditions affecting the time between paint jobs vary, but let's say you have to paint the house every five years. Assuming you are a do-it-yourselfer, capable of doing both painting and siding, how long will it take for the siding to pay for itself?

The first paint job will cost $400. If you elect to install siding, the job will cost $1,400. Subsequent paint jobs, for the sake of this example, will also cost $400, and they will be needed about every five years. Since the siding cost $1,000 more than the first paint job, you can repaint the house two and a half more times before you have spent the same amount of money. In other words, you would have to live in the house for the next seventeen years, roughly, to break even. If you factor in the power-washing of the vinyl siding, you might stretch the break-even point to twenty years.

Very few people stay in the same house for twenty years. So is vinyl siding a good deal? Well, you will have to be the judge of that question. Statistics suggest that vinyl siding can return up to about 70 percent of its initial cost, if the home is sold soon after the installation. Wood siding does better, by about 5 percent, in its rate of return.

If your home currently has a deteriorated siding material, for example, failing and peeling painted stucco, vinyl siding is probably your best option. You can cover the stucco, improve the looks of your home, add to its resale value, and most likely improve the home's heating/cooling efficiency.

In general, most contractors and appraisers agree that wood siding is more valuable and desirable than vinyl siding. However, in fairness, a lot of people prefer the limited maintenance associated with vinyl siding.

## STORM DOORS AND WINDOWS

Storm doors and windows are not as common as they once were. The current trend leans toward more efficient primary windows. Many people feel storm windows are ugly. Yet there are still plenty of contractors trying to sell their services to supply and install storm windows and doors.

Consumers are conscious of the costs of heating and cooling their homes, and storm windows and doors can reduce those costs. Since add-on windows and doors can save energy, they are worth considering.

### Storm Doors

Storm doors come in many designs, finishes, and prices. Low-end doors have prices starting at around $80. Better doors cost between $125 and $150, and premium doors can cost up to $250.

Patient homeowners can manage the installation of storm doors. If a professional installs your door, the labor charge will probably be around $100.

### Storm Windows

Storm windows are available in varying degrees of quality. Inexpensive units can be purchased for less than $30. Better windows are likely to run around $75. The price will fluctuate with the size of the window.

Installing storm windows is relatively easy. Any homeowner with average skills and tools can accomplish the task. Professionals, if installing a number of storm windows at the same time, will probably charge about $25 per unit.

Should you install storm windows and doors? You must weigh many factors to answer this question. Let's break these factors down into close-up details.

### Cost

Cost is certainly a consideration in fitting your home with storm windows and doors. Let's look at what the cost might be to equip our sample house. We will assume this house has two standard exterior doors and nine windows. If you use middle-of-the-road materials and do the installation yourself, the cost will be around $975. If you hire professionals to do the job, the cost might be $1,400.

If you already have high-quality primary windows and doors, the time it takes to recover your investment from energy savings could be substantial. However, if your primary windows and doors are not insulated and sealed tightly, the installation of storm windows and doors could pay for itself quickly.

As far as the value of storm windows and doors on an appraisal report, don't expect to see an increase of more than about 50 percent of the retail professional installation cost.

### Market Demand

Market demand can be a factor in your decision on whether or not to install storm windows and doors. If the homes surrounding yours are equipped with storm windows and doors, the investment is better justified than if the surrounding homes depend on only high-quality primary doors and windows for their energy savings.

## ROOFING

Roofing is usually more of a maintenance issue than an improvement issue. While some people do upgrade their roofing to a more distinguished material, most homeowners don't replace their roofs unless they have to.

Most homes are equipped with asphalt shingles, so that is the type of roof we will discuss. When it is time to put a new roof on your house, you have two options. You can have the new shingles applied over the old ones, or you can strip the roof down to its wood and start from scratch. Most building codes prohibit a roof having more than two layers of shingles. If your roof already has more than one layer of shingles, you should strip the roof of the old shingles before installing the new.

Asphalt shingles are sold in bundles, and it takes three bundles of shingles to cover 100 square feet. Like siding, a quantity of shingles capable of covering 100 square feet is called a square of shingles. A square of average shingles costs around $40.

If you assume you want to roof a house that requires fifteen squares of shingles, the shingles will cost $600. Drip edge, nails, and assorted minor expenses could add up to another $100.

Roofing over an existing roof requires much less work than stripping the roof of its old shingles and starting from raw wood. Even so, roofing can be dangerous, and it requires some special skills to get the shingles installed uniformly. Hiring professionals to roof over an existing roof will probably cost around $800 in labor. If they have to strip off the old roof, the labor rate could double.

Putting a new roof on your house is not a money-making investment. If you were to sell the house, you would probably recover less than half of your investment. However, if your roof needs to be replaced, ignoring the problem could result in a lower value for your home. If an appraiser sees the roof of a house must be replaced, the appraisal report is likely to be adjusted to allow for the anticipated cost of the maintenance.

### Other Types of Roofing

If you are thinking of installing another type of roofing material to increase the value of your home, think twice. Cedar shakes are very popular for new construction of certain styles of homes and in certain areas. However, they require regular treatment (every two or three years) for fireproofing, and homeowner's insurance premiums are likely to go up with the installation of cedar shakes. Cedar shakes are difficult to install; the typical do-it-yourselfer will split about as many shakes as he installs. This makes for a great deal of expensive waste.

Slate roofs are beautiful and nearly maintenance free. However, they are not suitable for remodeling. A slate roof is extremely heavy, weighing several tons, and must be installed on a foundation and roofing trusses built to support that weight.

## GUTTERS

Gutters are similar to storm windows in that they are practical but often considered an eyesore. Some people believe a house without gutters is naked, and others detest the look of gutters.

From a logical point of view, gutters are a good investment. A good rainwater system will control surface water around a home and can prevent some serious water-related problems. New gutter materials are available that are inexpensive and don't require routine painting. Screens can be placed over gutters to reduce maintenance headaches, and the right gutters do not detract from the beauty of most homes.

If you are interested in having gutters installed, be sure to plan what will happen to the water coming off your roof (Figure 4-1). If it is merely dumped out at the corners of your foundation, the gutters are not worth much. The downspouts should be tied into a drainage system that carries the water to a satisfactory disposal site.

Aluminum gutter material runs around $1.00 per linear foot. Some plastic gutters are less expensive. To install gutters and downspouts on our 44-foot house, the materials would cost around $125. This does not include labor or the materials for an underground drainage system.

Professional labor for installing the gutter on our sample house would probably be in the neighborhood of $400. All of these figures are based on installing gutters and downspouts on both the front and rear of the home.

As long as you are careful on your ladder and aware of any electrical wires in the area, installing gutters is not a hard job, but it does help to have an extra set of hands available.

The cost of an underground drainage system will depend on your local code requirements and soil conditions. The pipe used for the system is very inexpensive, but the digging can add up to a sore back, even though the trenches don't have to be deep.

Gutters add a little to the appraised value of your home, but it is not enough to consider the improvement an equity-builder. The main benefit of having gutters is the control of water that could damage your home.

There are, of course, other types of exterior projects that you may consider, but this chapter has dealt with the most common ones. The key to evaluating any improvement is research.

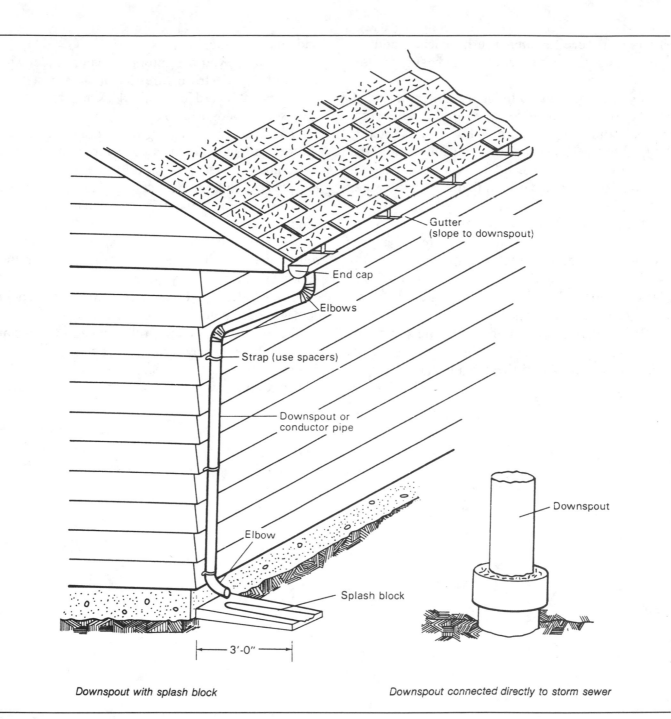

Downspout with splash block

Downspout connected directly to storm sewer

Figure 4-1. *Gutter installation. Courtesy of U.S. Dept. of Agriculture.*

# DECKS, PORCHES, AND SUNROOMS 5

Decks, porches, and sunrooms are all very popular home improvements. These improvements can be expensive. The more expensive an improvement is, the more important it is to be sure you are making a sound decision in proceeding with the project. This chapter concentrates on these three types of improvements. It will show you why building a big deck may be a financial flop when a deck of moderate size can be a great investment. You will see examples of just how much it will cost to build each of these projects.

After looking at the cost of these improvements, you will see how to rate the value of the various projects. All of these jobs have potential for building equity in your home, if you are willing to be your own general contractor. This chapter also gives comparisons to help you decide when the construction of a screened porch is a better choice than building a deck.

Before you finish this chapter, you will see how spending a little extra money on an enclosed porch or a sunroom can actually cost you less. That's right, there are times when spending more costs less, in a manner of speaking.

Unlike some of the improvements we have covered previously, all of these projects are likely to cost more than $1,000. In some cases, the retail values will go over $20,000. There can be big money at stake with any of these projects, but with the right planning, you can profit from these projects in increased equity.

We will begin our investigation with decks.

Then we will move on to porches; and finally, we will address sunrooms. The jobs are put in this order due to their typical retail values. We are starting at the bottom and working our way up.

## DECKS

Many homeowners add decks to their homes. Some have decks built as a place to congregate outside. The wooden platforms are used for cookouts, sunbathing, parties, and just plain relaxation. There are times decks are built to take advantage of a section of property that otherwise would not lend itself to personal enjoyment. A deck can turn a steep, practically unusable lawn into a level playground. With the proper railings and gate, a deck can be used as a safe place for children to be outdoors with minimal supervision.

A terraced deck can enhance the overall appearance of a home and create different levels of enjoyment. It is possible to use decks to conceal exterior mechanical equipment, but proper ventilation must be provided for any equipment housed under the deck. With the proper lighting, a deck can turn the night into an enchanted escape from the everyday world. There are many reasons for building decks, and many types of decks to consider building.

### Can You Build Your Own Deck?

Is it possible to build your own deck? Many homeowners do build their own decks. If the design you choose is not too complicated, there is a good chance you can build your own deck. Some designs and decking patterns make the job more difficult and suggest a need for professional construction. When the project is a one-level square or rectangular deck, construction requirements can be met by anyone with basic carpentry skills and tools. If, however, you elect to build a multi-level deck with octagonal platforms and built-in features, the skill level required may be beyond your capabilities.

If you are able to build your own deck, you have a good chance of building equity in your home. By being your own carpenter, the money you save in professional labor fees is funnelled into the equity you have in your home.

You can normally save money by acting as your own general contractor, but this may not be the case with deck construction. Being your own general contractor is most effective on large jobs and jobs where many trades are required. Since deck construction requires few trades and is usually a quick job, acting as your own general contractor may not save much money.

### How Much Does a Deck Cost?

How much will installation of a deck cost? The cost of a deck depends on many factors: size, design, types of materials used, site conditions, and labor rates. Since there are several variables in the cost of deck construction, let's look at some examples.

RECTANGULAR DECKS

Rectangular decks are the most common types of decks, and they are easier to build than more complex designs. For this example, we are going to build a rectangular deck with dimensions of 10' X 16'. We will use pressure-treated lumber and a pier foundation. To add to the deck's appearance and usefulness, we will build bench seating along two of the sides. In keeping the design simple, we will use horizontal boards for our safety railing.

The deck is going to attach to the side of your home, eliminating the need for foundation piers along the connecting edge. The edge that attaches to the home will be supported by a band board and ledger that is attached to the band board of the home. There will be a set of steps that descends to the backyard.

The cost of materials for this deck should be around $800. Breaking this down into a square-footage formula, we see the materials cost $5.00 per square foot.

If you build the deck yourself, you will probably invest between fifty and sixty hours of your time in the project. You can do the math to determine what your labor investment is worth in terms of dollars.

The size of our deck is 160 square feet. This is a good size for a deck, and it is a size that allows the maximum recovery of your investment. The appraiser I interviewed for this book would normally assign a value of $10 per square foot to a deck of this size. If we say the value of the deck is $1,600, your labor investment was worth $800 or between $13.33 and $16 an hour.

In this example, if you built the deck yourself, you built $800 of equity in your home. If you had a good time doing the work, you have increased your equity, satisfied yourself, and you have a deck to enjoy for years to come. Under this scenario, the project was very successful.

What would the deck have cost if professionals built it? Well, if I had sold you the deck, it would have cost about $1,900. In checking some estimating guides, you might see that the deck would cost close to $3,000 when built by professionals. The big variable is the cost of labor in your area.

If you will remember, I told you earlier in the book that I often found generic cost-estimating books to list labor costs at much higher rates than what I have seen to be common. This deck example is one of those times.

Carpenters in my area of Maine charge between $15 and $30 an hour. Carpenters with the proper licenses and insurance, who are fully established in business, will normally charge $25 an hour in my area.

In the case of the deck construction, much of the time spent on construction does not require extensive carpentry skills. For instance, six hours might be invested in digging the holes for the pier foundation, but this type of work doesn't require carpentry skills. A fair contractor would use a less skilled individual, at a lower hourly rate, to perform this type of work.

When you compare the number of hours of labor with the cost of labor in some estimating guides, you will find that the hourly labor rate is steep. Estimating guides are supposed to represent the cost of labor in your area. The guide will provide some conversion factor that allows you to arrive at a local labor rate.

Some estimating guides are better than others at projecting accurate costs. One of the guides I consult on occasion shows deck labor in my area at $38 an hour. While this is much higher than most contractors are really charging, it is not an unreasonable figure. The numbers I gave earlier for local labor rates were for small companies, often with just one carpenter. If a company with several crews and supervisors was bidding the deck construction, I would expect to see a labor rate of about $35 an hour.

If you are willing and able to provide your own labor in the construction of your deck, you can do very well on the project financially.

## L-Shaped Decks

L-shaped decks are more complicated than rectangular decks, but they are not so elaborate that handy homeowners cannot get the job done. In this cost example, we will maintain the same basic type of construction materials and practices used in the earlier example. The only differences will be the shape of the deck and increased square footage; this deck will have 224 square feet.

The cost of materials for this deck will run about $1,200. Putting the cost into a square-footage formula, we see the materials cost slightly more than those for the rectangular deck; these materials cost $5.35 per square foot. The additional costs are due to the shape of the deck.

This deck is of a size that still offers optimum return on your investment. The local appraiser I interviewed does not begin reducing square-footage value until a deck has more than 250 square feet of area. Under normal circumstances, the appraiser with whom I spoke would value this deck at $2,500. Keep in mind that the appraiser might allow more for the shape, bench seats, or other aspects of the deck. Since appraisals are based so heavily on conditions at individual locations, it is impossible to quote exact generic figures.

If you build this deck yourself, you might add $1,300 to the equity of your home. Again, if you enjoy the work, this is a great opportunity to add value to your home and gain a deck for your outside enjoyment.

While an L-shaped deck is not much harder to build than a rectangular one, the cost of labor for constructing this type of deck is likely to be higher. The shape slows down the construction process.

As a contractor, I would charge about $2,800 for this deck. I'm sure that as a homeowner, in my area, I could get the deck built by a professional carpenter for less than $2,400. On the other hand, I would not be surprised to see the job rated at $4,000 in a cost-estimating guide. These variances in retail costs are what makes it hard to determine the accuracy of resale statistics.

While you might find statistics that indicate a deck will be worth 60 percent of its value when a home is sold, you have to ask yourself how the statistics were derived. Another set of statistics could show the resale value of decks being 75 percent of their retail cost. Which set of statistics is right?

Knowing which statistics are the most accurate is not easy. While the numbers quoted in magazines, books, and reports are helpful, you cannot rely on them for your personal circumstances. To know where you stand on cost versus value, a local appraiser is your best source of information.

I mentioned earlier that the appraiser I talked with allows $10 per square foot for decks with sizes up to 250 square feet. Once the deck goes beyond that size, the value per square foot begins to drop. So while $10 to $12 per square foot is realistic for decks of average size and construction, this may be far too much to pay for a large, simple deck, and not nearly enough to cover the cost of a deck made from redwood. You must look at each project on an individual basis.

If you keep your deck at a reasonable size and use standard building materials (pressure-treated lumber), you have a good chance of recovering most if not all of your investment. Added to a sunroom, dining room, or family room, decks are attractive and useful (Figure 5-1).

## SCREENED PORCHES

Screened porches can provide a great deal of enjoyment. In areas where insects are abundant and decks see little use because of the bugs, screened porches provide an alternative. They allow you to enjoy the sounds, sights, and smells of being outside without the annoyance of biting insects. If it happens to be raining, you can enjoy sitting on your covered porch when sitting on an open deck would be a dampening experience. There are many reasons for considering the construction of a screened porch.

Is a screened porch a better improvement than a deck? The answer to this question depends upon whom you ask. The cost of a screened porch is more than twice that of a deck with similar dimensions, but the porch provides benefits the deck cannot. On the other hand, it is difficult to get a suntan while sitting on a screened porch. From a user's point of view, each improvement will have its pros and cons. From a value-versus-cost point of view, the two improvements are closely related. Let's explore this relationship further.

Screened porches can be built in a number of ways. They can have brick foundations and concrete floors. Porches can be built at ground level, on a concrete slab. The roof designs can range from simple shed roofs to more complicated hip roofs. The floor of the porch can be concrete, pressure-treated decking, indoor-outdoor carpet, slate, tile, or one of many other forms of floor covering. Electricity might be available in the porch, or the space can be a simple retreat from pesky insects. With so many possible options, the cost of a screened porch is not always easy to predict.

Since screened porches are not usually intended for year-round use, they are not normally considered an extension of a home's living space. This can cause trouble for the homeowner who invests too much in an elaborate screened porch. While a wet bar, ceiling fan, and weatherproof electrical outlets can be enjoyable, recovering their costs will not be easy. The same might be true of a brick foundation and poured floor that is covered with expensive quarry tile. If you want a screened porch, you will probably be better off, at least financially, to keep the structure simple.

For an example of how the cost and value of a basic screened porch compares, let's look at the figures for building a common screened porch. This porch is going to attach to the back of the house and be covered with a shed roof. It will have a pier foundation and the framing materials will be pressure-treated lumber. The exterior walls will be screened from floor to ceiling and screen will be in-

stalled under the floor joists, to prevent insect invasion from below. An electrical circuit will be installed to provide light and electrical outlets. The size of this porch will be the same as the rectangular deck in an earlier example: 160 square feet.

The construction of the porch foundation and flooring system will be very similar to that of the earlier deck. The big difference is in the roof structure and the screening. You will also need a screen door. The screening can be done with pre-fabricated panels, or you can use rolls of screen to cover the openings. The roof structure is a simple shed design that requires minimal materials.

Where the cost of materials for an open deck was $800, the cost of materials for this screened porch will run about $2,000. The cost of materials on a square-footage basis comes out to about $12.50. If it would take you fifty hours to build a deck of this size, it will probably take eighty hours to build the screened porch.

While the appraisal figures on the deck come in at $10 per square foot, the same type of formula used for a screened porch of this type might produce an estimated value of $25. So if we multiply 160 square feet by $25 a square foot, we arrive at a value of $4,000. By doing the work yourself, you could build as much as $2,000 in equity.

Hiring professionals to do the job for you will not produce such desirable results. This porch could easily cost $5,000 if it were built by a professional contractor.

The porch used in this example is larger than many screened porches, but it is not unreasonably large. It does, however, put the cost near the upper limits of strong recovery. The appraiser I interviewed felt that $3,500 was the most that should be invested in a screened porch, under normal circumstances. I chose to use this size in the example to make it easier to compare the screened porch to the deck.

If you want more than a basic screened retreat, consider building a sunroom. Putting a lot of money in half-walls, fancy flooring, and so forth in a screened porch is a high-risk investment.

## SUNROOMS

Sunrooms (Figures 5-2 and 5-3) can add living space to your home, make the home more appealing, and put equity in your home investment. Referred to as Florida rooms, sunrooms, solariums, and glass-enclosed porches, sunrooms are popular in most parts of the country.

Depending upon where they are built and how they are built, sunrooms can return most of the investment you make in them. If you do much of the work yourself, you can even earn a decent sum for your labor. By acting as your own general contractor, you should be able to enjoy a sunroom with no financial loss when you sell your home.

The potential costs for sunrooms range from less than $5,000 to well over $20,000. The size and degree of elegance inherent to sunrooms have much to do with their costs and values.

The appraiser with whom I consulted on this issue felt that under most conditions, in mid-coast Maine, an average sunroom would not rate more than $5,000. In contrast, when I was building sunrooms in Virginia, it was not unusual for them to appraise at more than twice that amount. It is also certainly feasible that a sunroom could appraise for much more than $5,000 in Maine. Keep in mind that the appraiser with whom I met was dealing with averages. If the sunroom is made a part of a home's living space, it could appraise for much more than if it is an unheated enclosed porch.

Some reports suggest that the average cost for sunrooms is around $25,000. Other statistics indicate that $15,000 is an average cost for a sunroom. Based on these costs, there is a common projection that sunrooms will return up to 70 percent of their value.

If you act as your own general contractor and save 20 percent of the total retail cost, you may only lose 10 percent of your acquisition cost. In other words, if you act as a general contractor for the construction of your Florida room, and the room has a retail value of $15,000, you may not lose more than $1,500 when you sell your house.

If you can do a large portion of the work yourself, you can actually make money by adding this improvement to your home. How much money can you net out of building your own sunroom? The amount will depend on how much of the work you do. To clarify this issue, let's look at some typical construction examples.

The range of possibilities for creating a sunroom is extensive. You can enclose the space with sliding glass doors, casement windows, pre-fabricated glass panels, and so forth. Each of these options will affect your cost. The type of flooring used in the space can make the price increase by hundreds of dollars. Even the choice of ceiling materials can have a significant effect on the overall price.

Will you install heat and air conditioning in the glass enclosure? If you do, the cost of the project will go up, but its value may increase by more than the cost of the installation of climate control. To keep our examples easy to follow, we will use standard materials and normal construction practices.

## The Sliding Glass Door Approach

The sliding glass door approach is an easy method for a homeowner to use in building a sunroom. With basic carpentry skills, like those used to build a screened porch, a homeowner can handle this type of project. Since the glass doors are stock items in building supply stores, the cost of materials will be moderate. Fixed-glass panels are less expensive, but they do not allow ventilation as the sliding glass doors do.

Our sample sunroom will contain about 192 square feet. Its dimensions, in round numbers, will be 12' X 16'. This size allows us to use two 6-foot door units on each end and two 8-foot door units on the wide wall. The fourth wall is attached to the home and opens into the living space.

Most real estate professionals agree that sunrooms are most effective when they open into a dining room, kitchen, or family room.

The first consideration is the type of foundation to use. You could use a pier foundation and pressure-treated posts for the support of your room's floor. A monolithic slab might be a cost-effective floor, but it could make the job of getting heat, air conditioning, and plumbing to the space more difficult. A brick or block foundation could be used, but the cost of materials will be more. Maybe a poured concrete foundation wall would be best. Which type of foundation should you use?

The decision on the best type of foundation will depend, to some degree, on the style of your home and the standard practices in your area. If you have a home with contemporary styling and a natural wood exterior, a pier foundation, which is concealed with lattice, might be the best foundation choice.

Houses with brick foundations tend to call for a brick foundation under the Florida room. If your house is built on a slab foundation, then a slab foundation for the sunroom would be fine.

Once you have established what type of foundation and subflooring to use, the next question is the roof. A shed roof is easy to build and inexpensive. For most house designs, a shed roof looks fine on a Florida room.

There are, of course, other details to work out. You have to decide how much of the exterior wall of your home to remove. Will you have just a door into the glass enclosure, or will you remove a section of the existing exterior wall to make the house appear brighter and larger? The best answer to this question will depend on many circumstances, but if you can open up a section of the existing exterior wall, the addition of your Florida room will be much more impressive.

As you can see, the decision to build a sunroom is not one that you can make lightly. There are many elements of your existing home that must be considered, and the project can be quite complicated.

Now that we have some of the rules set, let's see how much this sun space is going to cost. Let's assume you are going with an 8-inch concrete foundation wall and a wood-frame floor.

The cost of materials is difficult to project since we are not working with a complete set of plans and specifications, but it is safe to assume the cost will be around $6,000. This works out to be $31.25 per square foot, but your actual costs could be much more, depending on the types of materials used.

If the materials cost $6,000 and you do all the work yourself, you are going to build significant equity in your home. Let's assume the retail value of the sunroom is set at $65 a square foot; the retail price of this project is $12,480. By doing the work yourself, you will have earned about $6,000 in equity for your time. If you act as your own general contractor, you might earn $2,500 in equity.

It is, however, unlikely that you possess all the skills needed to complete the addition of a sunroom without professional help. Some of the areas with which average homeowners are likely to have the most trouble are the foundation, electrical wiring, and drywall finishing. The design of your space will influence what trades are needed.

Before you run out to contract the construction of a Florida room, be advised: it would not be unusual for a fancy Florida room to be priced at more than $100 per square foot. Due to the large spread in the cost of materials, your sunroom could have a retail price of anywhere between $50 and $125 per square foot.

## Construction Options

There are many construction options available for sunrooms. Casement windows are often favored because they can be opened to allow full ventilation. Unlike sliding glass doors that open for only one-half their total width, casement windows open fully.

Fixed glass is an inexpensive material to use in building a sunroom, but since the glass cannot be opened, the room loses some of its potential value.

Sliding glass doors are common, near a mid-range in expense, and well accepted. But there are many people who want the lower sections of wall space in a sunroom to be made from materials other than glass. In addition, the space required to open and close sliding glass doors can limit furniture placement.

Molded greenhouse panels that curve at the top are popular, but most of these panels don't allow the option of ventilation. Since the curved design forms a glass roof, a panel's extra cost is offset, to some extent, in the savings of other building materials.

Before you invest thousands of dollars in a sunroom, do plenty of research. Find out what the trends are in your area and don't build a non-conforming addition. The money required to build a sunroom, even if you do all the work yourself, is considerable, and without the proper research you could easily lose half of your investment.

This chapter has introduced you to three types of improvements that when done properly can increase the equity you have in your home. We are about to move on to Chapter Six and see how a room addition, another type of equity-building improvement, can be built while allowing you to increase your home's equity by thousands of dollars. If you like the idea of tackling a big project, turn the page and explore the world of room additions.

Figure 5-1. *This deck opening out of the dining area adds a feeling of spaciousness. Courtesy of Velux-America, Inc.*

Figure 5-2. *This sunroom incorporates skylights, a ceiling fan, and the typical large expanses of glass to bring the outdoors in. Courtesy of Velux-America, Inc.*

Figure 5-3. *A smaller sunroom in a more traditional style. Courtesy of Velux-America, Inc.*

# ROOM ADDITIONS

Room additions can cost well over $30,000. Even with their expensive price tag, room additions are common home improvements. People add on to their homes when they need more space but don't want, or are not able, to move. Some people build room additions to gain the benefit of space they want, whether they need it or not. In addition to these two groups of people, homeowners build room additions to build equity in their homes.

Room additions can be excellent equity-building improvements, but they can also be high-risk investments. If you build the right type of addition and act as your own general contractor, you can recover all of your cash investment. When you do some of the work yourself, you can turn a profit. If increased equity is your goal, adding a room addition to your home can increase your equity by thousands of dollars.

Whether you are contemplating a room addition out of necessity or desire, this chapter is going to help you make intelligent decisions on the subject. You will see what types of additions are the safest bets, and how to make the most of these high-dollar home improvements.

## What Types of Room Additions are Worth Considering?

What types of room additions (Figure 6-1) should you consider? Bedrooms, bathrooms, family rooms, and dining rooms are some of the most common types of room additions, and all of these types can be worth your consideration. Not only are full room additions worth considering, you might want to look at

your options for expanding your kitchen. Let's look at these different types of additions in detail.

BEDROOMS

Bedrooms are usually added because of need. As families expand, they need more bedrooms. Bedrooms are sometimes added to make a small house more compatible with other homes in the neighborhood. When a bedroom is added out of pure desire, it is often a master bedroom suite. All of these reasons can be good reasons for adding a bedroom. The decision to add this type of space should be examined closely.

If your home is in an area where most homes have three bedrooms, adding to your house to create five bedrooms will almost always be a financial mistake. It will be difficult to recover the cost of your improvement when the home is sold.

If you own a two-bedroom home and want to add a third bedroom to make more space or to be more in keeping with the other homes in the area, your improvement dollars may be a wise investment. It is important, however, not to overlook other aspects of your home. If the house was originally built as a two-bedroom home and you add bedrooms, you may find that the home is not functional.

By increasing the number of bedrooms, you increase the sleeping capacity of the house, but you may need to alter the kitchen, bathroom, or other rooms in the house to allow for the increased occupancy. This is a trap many homeowners fall into. They can get by with just one bathroom or a tiny kitchen, but when they try to sell their house, the public doesn't want a house that is not sized proportionally. In addition, real estate appraisers will take a dim view of property that is not up to par.

Adding an expansive master bedroom can be good for your personal enjoyment, but it may not be a wise investment. Just as in the comments above, adding a master bedroom suite complete with bathroom will increase the investment you have in your home but may not increase its market value proportionally.

Can you imagine being a home buyer and walking into a home where the original home contained less than 1,000 square feet and the new bedroom addition contains 300 square feet? Don't you think it would be a little odd to have a bedroom suite that was nearly as large as a third of the rest of the house? This type of improvement is not likely to be a good investment.

With any type of addition, you must assess all angles of how the improvement will affect your home. If you hope to recover most of your improvement cost, you must make sure that the market will support your improvement and that the public will agree with your decisions in the improvement.

## BATHROOMS

Bathrooms (Figure 6-2) are said to be one of the two most important rooms in a house when it comes to selling the property. Many older homes have only one bathroom. With today's changing lifestyles, there is a demand for multiple bathrooms, even in relatively small homes.

Adding a bathroom can not only make your life more enjoyable, it can build equity in your home and result in a cash profit if you decide to sell your house. There are, however, rules to follow when adding a bathroom. You will learn all about what makes a bathroom addition a sound investment a little later in the chapter.

## FAMILY ROOMS

Family rooms (Figure 6-3) are probably the most popular type of room addition built out of desire. People want a room to relax in, and parents want their children to have a comfortable place to play. Family rooms can meet both of these needs, and generally are good investments. There are, of course, serious considerations to think over before

spending $25,000 for any type of addition, and you will see how they pertain to family rooms shortly.

## DINING ROOMS

Formal dining rooms are not as common as they once were, but many people still like the concept. Some prefer a formal room with less formal furniture (Figure 6-4), a modified formal look; and other people favor a full formal look. If your home has only an eat-in kitchen, adding a dining room might be one of the home improvements on your mind. Adding a formal dining room is more risky than some of the other types of room additions, but a contemporary dining room might fit in nicely (Figure 6-5). The reasons for this increased risk are explained later in the chapter.

## KITCHEN EXPANSION

Kitchen expansion is sometimes the only way to make an existing kitchen work the way you want it to. Small kitchens can be a problem, and many homes have kitchens that don't cater to cooks. If you are thinking about enlarging your kitchen, you have a chance to make a safe investment and get a good return on the venture. Many people expand their kitchens to incorporate a spacious dining area and develop a country kitchen theme (Figure 6-6). Kitchens enjoy the prestige of being the most important rooms in homes being sold. While many statistics and reports on the best home improvements and the costs and values of home improvements conflict, all seem to agree that kitchens are a great place to deposit your home-improvement dollars.

## THE PROS AND CONS OF ROOM ADDITIONS

What are some of the positive and negative aspects of room additions? There are many good reasons for adding space to your home, but there are also some negative aspects to spending large sums of money adding on to your home. To make this comparison clear, let's look at some of the pros and cons.

### Benefits

There are benefits to be had when you add space to your home. The right addition, built the right way at the right time, can add value to your home in an amount greater than your expense. Since most people enjoy making money, this can be a strong benefit. You must be aware, however, that not all additions are profitable.

Personal enjoyment of your increased living area is a benefit that has value, but it is a value each individual must put his or her own price tag on.

Building an addition to your home can make the house easier to sell. If you plan to sell your house, this can be a great advantage.

Houses usually appreciate in value year after year. The rate of appreciation varies with the economy, but appreciation rates are a percentage of your home's total value. Meaningful additions will allow your home to grow in value when they are built, and they will continue to help your home's value grow through appreciation. Let's look at an example of how this can work to your advantage.

Let's assume you own a house that is worth $100,000. If we pick an annual appreciation rate of 5 percent, your house should increase in value by 5 percent every year that you own it. The increased value would look like this:

| | |
|---|---|
| Year one: | $100,000 |
| Year two: | $105,000 |
| Year three: | $110,250 |
| Year four: | $115,762.50 |
| Year five: | $121,550.62 |

Your five-year gain in value would amount to $21,550.62.

Now assume you added a $25,000 family room to the house when you bought it. The house you bought for $100,000 is worth $125,000 after the addition of the family room. With the same 5 percent appreciation rate, your equity gain would look like this:

| | |
|---|---|
| Year one: | $125,000 |
| Year two: | $131,250 |
| Year three: | $137,812.50 |
| Year four: | $144,703.12 |
| Year five: | $151,938.27 |

Your five-year gain in value would amount to $26,938.27. The addition of the family room allowed you to earn $5,387.65 that would not have been gained without the addition; this is an equity gain of about $1,000 per year.

This example does not take into account the extra real estate taxes you would probably have to pay on your home, but it still shows that the increased value offered by the room addition continues to work for you over the years.

**Disadvantages**

What are the disadvantages of adding a room addition to your home? Room additions are expensive, and that can be a disadvantage. Spending $25,000 for a family room could put a strain on your cash reserves or your monthly budget.

If you make poor decisions in the construction of your addition, you could be investing money that will never be recovered. Not all room additions allow a strong recovery of the initial investment. Some examples of poor room additions include:

- a room paneled in dark materials and with little natural light

- too-small bedrooms (any room addition should be at least 8' x 10'; smaller could only be a nursery or possibly a sewing room)

- an overly fancy formal dining room with chair rail, high grade carpeting, crystal chandelier, and expensive wall treatment (only for the highest level homes)

- an exercise room

- any addition with poor quality or craftsmanship (the "do-it-yourselfer" look)

If you are trying to sell your home, you might find that the $25,000 you spent on a family room the year before has priced your house out of the market. It may be that the house would sell without the family room at a lower price, but that buyers are not willing, or able, to pay the extra amount for the room addition. This could be extremely frustrating.

## WHAT ROOM ADDITION SHOULD I BUILD?

What room addition is best to build? A blanket statement cannot be made that will work for all people in all places. Generally, kitchen expansions rate the highest in the amount of value returned and in public appeal. Bathrooms typically fall into second place on such a list, and other additions make up the remainder of the list. Whether a family room is a better bet than a master bedroom depends on the house being improved, comparable houses in the area, and market demand. To determine which improvements have the best chance of financial success, you must assess your local market conditions.

If you are building a room addition because you need one, you will know what type of room should be built, but you must decide if it is wiser to build an addition or to move up to a larger home. You may be in a position where adding space to your existing home would be a financial mistake. Sometimes it is better to sell the house you own and buy a larger one.

Now that the groundwork is laid and you understand a little about how various room additions can affect your home's value, let's look at the cost of some of these additions.

### Simple Bedroom Additions

Simple bedroom additions are one of the least expensive types of room additions to build. These rooms don't require any plumbing, and they have minimal needs for heating, cooling, and electrical increases. Bedroom additions don't have to be large to be effective, and there are no expensive cabinets, countertops, or fixtures involved in the job.

A bedroom doesn't have to be large, but it should contain at least 80 square feet and a closet. (Appraisers frequently require that, for a room to be categorized as a bedroom, it have a closet.) For our example of cost, we will use a bedroom with 96 square feet; its dimensions are 8' X 12'. There will be nothing fancy about this addition, but it will be built to standards that allow a full appraised value.

The cost of materials for such an addition should be around $2,600. This works out to a cost of $27 per square foot for materials. Professional labor to build the addition might cost between $3,500 and $4,500. If you say the combined cost of labor and materials would be $6,000, the cost per square foot would be $62.50. As always, keep in mind that these figures are for illustration only and may vary.

How much is this bedroom worth? If your family is growing quickly, the bedroom might be worth $10,000 to you, but it won't have that much value on

an appraisal. The value of an added bedroom will depend on how many bedrooms your home had prior to the addition and how many bedrooms other homes in the area have.

If your home needed the extra bedroom to compete with comparable properties, you may see the value of your home increased by the amount invested in the bedroom. For example, if homes in your area typically have three or four bedrooms and you have only two, you will gain quite a bit of value by adding a bedroom. If, however, the bedroom addition gives your home more bedrooms than the surrounding homes have, you may not gain enough equity to cover the cost of the job.

Appraisers normally work their appraisals with many different formulas. For example, an appraiser may use a square-footage formula to arrive at the value of your bedroom, but this would not normally be the only measurement of value. Your room could be assigned a lump-sum value for being a bedroom. The cost of construction would be evaluated, and comparable sales and market demand would be examined.

When you are building a small addition, like the bedroom in this example, the cost per square foot is usually high. It is conceivable that this bedroom could cost $80 per square foot to build. If the room was being built at the same time the rest of the house was being constructed, the cost would be much lower. This can cause a problem when you are hoping to recover your construction costs.

Appraisers must look at the value of your home, not the fact that your three-bedroom house cost more than your neighbor's because you had to add the third bedroom as an addition and your neighbor's home was built originally with three bedrooms. Before you spend a lot of money on major home improvements, you should invest in a before-and-after appraisal to assess the value of the improvement.

### Master Bedroom Suites

Master bedroom suites, even small ones, that contain bathrooms can get expensive fast. Adding a bathroom in the addition runs the cost up quickly, and may not be worthwhile. If your home will benefit from an extra bathroom, the cost might be justified. But if the bathroom is for pure convenience and is not needed to make your house more competitive with comparable properties, it may be a money-losing proposition.

The materials for an addition with dimensions of 12' X 16', which will contain a bedroom and a bathroom, may cost $6,500. On a square-footage basis, this is $33.85 per square foot for materials. Adding the bathroom to the addition normally means paying a plumber, and you know how much money plumbers are supposed to make. The labor cost for all trades involved in this type of project may run between $6,500 and $8,500.

Your total cost for this addition might average out at $14,000. The cost per square foot would work out to about $73. This is $10 per square foot more than the bedroom addition without the bathroom. If you decide to build the addition without the bathroom, the overall cost should drop by about $2,500. This would put your square-footage cost at just under $60.

The cost of this job could shoot up to $17,000 if you decide to use upgraded carpeting, wallpaper, fancy fixtures, and ornate trim in the bathroom.

I know I've said it over and over, but I want to remind you that it is imperative for you to check prices in your own area before making any decision. Generic cost guides are helpful, and my experience can tell you a lot, but only first-hand investigation at the time of your action will be accurate.

## Bathroom Additions

Bathroom additions carry a heavy per-square-foot cost. The relatively small rooms are filled with plumbing, and plumbing is expensive.

When it comes to return on investment, bathrooms rank high on the list of best jobs. Even with their high costs, bathrooms have a strong track record for recovering their costs. Statistics show that you can recover anywhere from 50 percent to 200 percent of your investment in a bathroom addition.

I would question whether you can see a 200 percent return, but I don't doubt for a minute that you can recover 100 percent of your investment, even if you hire out all of the work. While you can often cover your cash expenses in other forms of improvements by being your own general contractor or by doing the work yourself, it is rare to find an improvement that allows you to pay full retail price

and still recover all of your money. Bathroom additions offer this unique possibility. Don't misconstrue these words, building a bathroom addition doesn't guarantee success. The addition must be necessary, and it must be built properly.

### POWDER ROOMS

A powder room (half bath) can sometimes be added by converting a closet or making use of space under a staircase. If you can add a bathroom within the walls of your existing home, your costs will be much less than if you must build an exterior addition. Powder rooms don't command as much value as full bathrooms, but they do appeal to people and increase your home's value.

According to the appraiser I with whom I consulted with on this book, the addition of a powder room within the confines of your existing home should result in an increased value equal to 100 percent of your improvement investment.

If you have a spare closet that can be converted into a half bath, the cost for the project, even if you hire professionals to supply the materials and labor, should be less than $3,000. If you keep the conversion simple and shop for the best prices on labor and materials, you might get by with a cost of $2,000.

If you decide to do the conversion yourself, the plumbing fixtures can be bought for less than $300. You will need an exhaust fan and some light fixtures, but these items should cost less than $150. The rest of what will be needed depends on your preference, but it is possible to buy all the materials needed for converting a closet into a powder room for less than $750. When you consider that the powder room will probably be worth $2,500, this is a good opportunity for you to pick up some extra equity.

### FULL BATHROOMS

Full bathrooms are more difficult to fit into closets. The space requirements for a full bath are usually a minimum of 35 square feet, and normal dimensions, at their smallest, are 5' X 7'. If you are making a new space for a bathroom, you would do well to make the bathroom larger.

Let's look at an example of what it might cost to build a bathroom addition with dimensions of 8' X 8'. A bathroom of this size would allow plenty of room for all the plumbing fixtures and a vanity area.

The cost of materials for such a bathroom would be around $3,200. Professional labor to build the addition might run an extra $6,000. With good negotiating skills and intense shopping, you might get a package price as low as $7,500. At the upper end, the cost per square foot is $143, and at the bargain price, the cost per square foot is $117. As you can see, the cost per square foot is substantial. While you will rarely go wrong by adding a powder room or full bath within your existing walls, you could get in over your head by building a full-blown addition.

In watching trends and reports from across the country, I have seen bathroom additions of modest proportions range in price from about $8,000 all the way up to $15,000. Average prices seem to be around $10,000, and even at these numbers, the improvements return an average of 95 percent of their cost.

### Family Room Additions

Family room additions (Figure 6-7) are popular, and they can offer a good return on your investment. If you are willing to act as your own general contractor, you should be able to recover all of your cash investment from a family room addition.

Family rooms can be made to any size, but it is often recommended that they contain at least 400 square feet and be flooded with natural light. This may seem like a lot of room if you live in a small house, but if you make the room too small, it will be little more than a spare bedroom.

To get an idea of costs, let's look at a big family room, one with dimensions of 20' X 24'. The material costs for this type of project are in the neighborhood of $13,000. Adding the cost of professional contractors, including a general contractor, the total cost might hit $30,000. The price could, of course, be more or less.

At a per-square-foot cost of $62.50, a family room of this size is a big investment, but the cost is reasonable. National averages of large family rooms may run around $70 per square foot.

How will this addition stack up in value? You should recover between 60 and 85 percent of the total retail value. Some opinions on this type of investment are better than others. While statistics show moderate to strong recovery on this type of investment, the appraiser with whom I spoke was not

so optimistic; her projections dipped as low as a 45 percent return. Let me say, however, that the appraiser was dealing only with local conditions and values.

### Dining Room Additions

The cost of a dining room addition is similar to that of a family room addition, but the return on your investment may not be as good. Since the demand for a formal dining room is not as great as the demand for a family room, the rate of recovery on a dining room project might only be around 50 percent. This type of addition should be approached with caution and extensive research.

### Expanding a Kitchen

The cost of expanding a kitchen is very difficult to project on a generic basis. The cost of kitchen cabinets alone can be enough to distort the projections by thousands of dollars.

We are going to talk about kitchen remodeling in detail in Chapter 13, but while we are on the subject of additions, I will attempt to give you some feel for the cost of kitchen expansion.

A major kitchen remodeling job, without adding onto your house, could cost $20,000. You have seen through the many examples the cost of adding space to a house. Trying to put the pieces of the pricing puzzle together in an estimate will result, at best, in a primitive guess.

If we assume you are going to add 100 square feet of space to your kitchen, by way of an outside addition, your cost will probably range from $20,000 to $35,000. I have seen cost statistics that put remodeling costs in excess of $40,000; so you might hit $50,000 by including additional space. Will you recover this cost? I doubt it.

Kitchen remodeling is one of the safest home improvements you can do, but adding space with an addition runs the cost up to the point where you stand to lose money. Before you make a major monetary investment in adding a little space to your kitchen, talk with local professionals and research the market trends in your area.

We are now done with this chapter on room additions and ready to move on to the next chapter. Chapter 7 is going to show you how to assess the costs and values of garages and carports.

Figure 6-1. *This room addition could be a study, guest room, sewing room—you choose. Courtesy of Lis King Public Relations and Curtron.*

**Figure 6-2.** *A spacious and elegant bathroom addition. Courtesy of Mannington resilient floors.*

Figure 6-3. *The hardwood floors and brick fireplace of this family room addition add value and style to the home. Courtesy of Azrock Industries, Azrock Floor Products.*

Figure 6-4. *A dining room addition of the style shown could prove a good value—not too formal, not so small as to be inefficient. Courtesy of Azrock Industries, Azrock Floor Products.*

Figure 6-5. *This contemporary dining room addition has lots of style and lots of light. Courtesy of Velux-America, Inc.*

Figure 6-6. *The country theme of this kitchen extends naturally into the dining room addition. Courtesy of Lis King Public Relations and The Colonial Williamsburg Foundation.*

Figure 6-7. *A more elegant family room addition opening to the outdoors. Courtesy of Velux-America, Inc.*

# GARAGES AND CARPORTS

Garages and carports are both common after-market add-ons, with garages being the more popular of the two. Carports are not as prolific as they once were, but garages seem to be growing in popularity. People like the many functions garages can serve.

Garages are intended to house vehicles, but they are often used for other purposes. They are frequently used to store items not wanted in a home, and they are sometimes given to the pursuit of hobbies. It is not unusual to find a garage so filled with model trains or woodworking equipment that a car could never be placed under the roof.

There are times garages serve dual purposes. The lower level of these garages can be used to shelter the family car, while the converted attic provides a studio, a guest room, or even an apartment. There are indeed many potential uses for a garage.

Carports are much more limited in their capacity to serve multiple purposes. A carport provides overhead shelter, but since this structure is not enclosed on the sides and ends, it cannot come close to offering the benefits of a garage. A carport is, however, much less expensive to construct than a garage, and it does provide some protection for vehicles or stacks of firewood.

If you are thinking of building a garage or a carport, there are some questions you should consider. One of the most important questions could have to do with the zoning regulations in your area. Zoning regulations can restrict where you place structures on your property.

## ZONING REGULATIONS, COVENANTS AND RESTRICTIONS

While you may own more than enough land to accommodate a new garage, you may be prevented by zoning regulations from building one. Don't build any type of structure without first checking local ordinances and obtaining the proper permits.

Deed restrictions and covenants may also limit what you can build on your property. If your home is located in a planned community, it is very likely that there are some restrictions pertaining to outside structures. For example, you may be allowed to build a garage but not a carport. The covenants and restrictions may require that all garages built within the community be of certain dimensions or styles. You might even be limited in the type of siding you may use or the color you may paint your new garage. These types of restrictions may appear harsh, but they do exist in some locations.

## SIZE OF THE GARAGE OR CARPORT

Another question to ask yourself might deal with the size or your garage or carport. If all the homes in your neighborhood have two-car garages, your home would look out of place with a three-car garage. Building a one-car garage could hurt your chances of a quick sale if you ever decide to sell your home.

If you are thinking of a garage, you must decide whether it will be attached to your home or detached. Will the method of attachment be direct or by way of a breezeway? What type of roof and what roof pitch best suit your needs? There is much to consider before digging a foundation.

As with most tangibles in life, cost is a factor in your final decision. How much does it cost to build a one-car garage? Does it cost twice as much to build a two-car garage? How much money can you save by settling for a carport?

Let's take a look at what it will cost to build these types of shelter for your vehicle.

## CARPORTS

Carports are the least expensive form of shelter you can build for your car. There are several possible variations on the construction of a carport. The structure might be nothing more than a metal roof supported by a few posts, or it may have a concrete slab, a stick-built roof, and attractive lattice on the sides. Obviously, the costs of these two versions are considerably different.

### Simple One-Car Carport

If you are going to build a carport, keep it simple. Opt for a roof supported by posts and little more. If you go to the expense of installing a slab and complete privacy screens, you might as well build a garage.

Let's assume you are going to build a one-car attached carport. You are going to use a shed roof, support posts, and a privacy screen on the side wall. The cost of materials for this type of job will run about $800. This will give you a carport with dimensions of 12' X 22'.

If you hire a general contractor to erect the structure for you, the total cost might run $2,000. If you are at all handy, this type of project is simple and goes up quickly. Doing the job yourself, you can have a nice carport for less than $1,000.

As long as the carport is not competing against garages at neighboring houses, it should hold its value well.

### Two-Car Carport

Suppose you want a free-standing two-car carport, how much will that cost? Assume you will build a 24' X 22' carport. Materials for such a structure are likely to cost $1,500. Professional labor

might add another $2,000 to the cost, giving you a total cost of $3,500.

The cost of this carport is less than that of a garage, but the price is high enough that it may be hard to recover. If you do the work yourself, you should be fine, but hiring professionals may cause you to lose money on the project when your house is sold.

## SINGLE-CAR GARAGES

Single-car garages are not as popular as two-car garages, but they do rate higher than carports. They are also more expensive than carports. What does a one-car attached garage cost? Let's find out.

Our sample garage will have dimensions of 12' X 22'. It will attach to the side of the home and be fitted with a gable roof. The use of a shed roof could be substituted to reduce costs, but the gable roof will often look better. This garage will have one window and a 9' X 7' garage door.

The cost of materials for our sample garage should come to about $3,000. If professionals are hired to do the job, the total cost might land between $6,000 and $8,000. This is a lot of money to pay for a single-car garage. If you do the job yourself, your odds of breaking even are good, but if you hire professionals, you are probably going to lose some money.

## TWO-CAR GARAGES

Two-car garages are by far the most popular form of shelter for automobiles. These buildings can be constructed to provide substantial living space over the parking area. With the right roof design, it is possible to create a one-bedroom apartment in the upper level of a two-car garage.

A standard size for this type of garage is 24' X 24', and that is the size we are going to look at for construction costs. Our sample garage will have two windows, a standard entry door, and a garage door with dimensions of 16' X 7'. The garage will be detached from the home.

The materials for this garage should be priced around $4,000—only $1,000 more than the materials for a one-car attached garage. The cost of hiring a general contractor to build this garage for you might be $12,000. The price could even be as low as $5,000, if you believe some of the advertisements you see.

How can there be such a spread in the cost of a two-car garage? Regional differences have some impact on price, but most of the variation is in labor. Of course, the quality of materials and workmanship also affects the cost.

What is a detached two-car garage worth? I sold a lot of them for between $10,000 and $12,000 when I was working in Virginia. In Maine, the appraiser I spoke to gave an estimated value of $7,500 for an average two-car garage. There are ads running here in Maine every week offering people complete two-car garages for less than $5,000. Pricing guides indicate a cost in the area of $11,000 for the same garage. So where does this leave us in pegging the real value? It leaves us confused.

I can tell you from experience that a three-person crew can complete the construction of a 24' X 24' garage in less than seven days. Two of the people in the crew are accomplished carpenters and one of the workers is a helper. Let's do a little math and see what the truth might be.

The cost of materials is easy enough to determine, and $4,000 is a good ballpark estimate for average materials. Now, let's put the cost of labor under a microscope and see what we can discover.

Figuring the worst case of my past experience, it would not take more than two weeks for a three-person crew to complete our sample garage. If we figure a labor charge of $35 per hour for each of the two carpenters and $20 per hour for the helper, we come up with a total hourly fee of $90. When we multiply $90 times eighty hours, we arrive at a figure of $7,200. Adding $4,000 for materials, we come out at $11,250. This number is so close to what estimating guides predict that it's scary.

Now if I know from experience that the price of a detached two-car garage should fall between $10,000 and $12,000, and respected pricing guides put the cost between $11,000 and $12,000, how can anyone sell this type of garage for $5,000? I'll answer that question shortly.

Are you wondering why an experienced real estate appraiser would rate this garage at only $7,500? The appraiser I talked with was talking in terms of resale values, not the costs of construction. When

she said the garage would be worth about $7,500, she was talking about the garage's value to a home buyer in mid-coast Maine. This would indicate that our sample garage would recover about 70 percent of its retail cost when the property was sold. So the appraiser was very accurate in her figures. But that still leaves us with those contractors offering to build the same garage for $5,000.

Can anyone build a garage for $5,000 and stay in business? It's possible, but what will you get for your money? Let's look at the labor issue again, except this time we will look at it on a different level. The earlier example was based on a company where crews did the work, supervisors supervised the work, and the general contractor took care of administrative duties. In other words, the labor rates had to cover overhead expenses.

Suppose you had two brothers working together to build the garage. This partnership of brothers would have no employees and very low overhead. If they were real go-getters, they could complete the garage in a week, but they would probably have to work more than forty hours. But if they worked hard all week, even at a sales price of only $5,000, each brother would make $500.

Now $500 a week is not a lot of money for skilled tradesmen, but in rough economic times, it is better than not having a job at all. The contractors running the low-ball ads could be operating on one of many objectives.

They could be laid off from their regular jobs and trying to put food on the table. While you can't blame anyone for wanting to survive, as a consumer, you must wonder what the chances are that the workers will honor warranty calls if you have problems a month down the road. The crew that built your garage may have moved to another state to find stable work, and then you are left with a problem and no one to fix it.

The advertisements may be showing low numbers to get a salesperson in your house. If you respond to the ad, a skilled salesperson may come over to give you an estimate, but wind up selling you the "Deluxe Model" at a much higher price.

Materials are another way any contractor can cut the cost of building the garage. The savings might be passed on to you in the form of a lower price, or the contractor might keep the extra profits.

Here are a few quick examples of how materials can make a big difference.

If I use particleboard sheathing for your roof instead of plywood, I might be able to cut the cost of my sheathing materials in half. If I use an uninsulated aluminum sliding window instead of a standard double-hung window, I might save $150 per window. It is very possible I could sell you a cheap garage door and pocket an extra $300. If you start to add up all the ways to hack and slash material prices, I could come up with perhaps a $1,000 savings in material. If those two brothers did this, they would each be making $1,000 a week, so maybe they aren't desperate, but slick.

If I were you, I would plan on spending about $20 per square foot for a well-built, detached two-car garage. By doing the work yourself, you can build several thousand dollars of equity in your home. Should you choose to spend your money with an econo-model, let the buyer beware.

Now let's move on to Chapter 8 and see how you will make out if you decide to install replacement windows and doors.

# WINDOW AND DOOR REPLACEMENT 8

If you watch television, listen to radio broadcasts, or receive mail, you must have heard of replacement windows and doors. This is one home improvement that gets plenty of advertising. Are replacement windows as good as their sellers say they are? Can replacing your front door reduce your heating and cooling costs? Both of these questions can be answered with one word: yes.

Replacement windows and doors are viable home improvements, and they can save you money on your heating and cooling costs. They can also improve the appearance and desirability of your home. Is there anything else you should know about replacement windows and doors? You bet there is, and this chapter is going to tell you what you need to know.

## GOOD LOOKS

Good looks are one reason for installing replacement windows and doors. The windows and doors on the front of your house play an important role in the appearance of your home. If your existing windows and doors are dilapidated, your house will not look its best.

While wanting your house to look good is one reason for replacing the windows and doors in your home, it is not the reason most people choose this home improvement. Replacement windows are expensive, and most houses can have their old windows spruced up with a little paint and attention. Since replacing windows only to obtain a better

look is usually cost-prohibitive, you need an additional reason for parting with your hard-earned money. What better reason could you have to spend money than to save money? Well, that's the main reason so many people invest in replacement windows. They are looking for energy savings that will translate into cash savings.

## ENERGY SAVINGS

Energy savings are the main motivation for most buyers of replacement windows and doors. The promise of reduced energy costs is a good selling point for replacement windows and doors. The potential for saving money is such a good selling point that many people buy replacement windows without ever considering how long they will have to keep their house to recover their investment.

Deciding if you should spend thousands of dollars on windows that are supposed to save you money should be a serious decision, but not all homeowners see it that way. Many homeowners pay more than they should for replacement windows and never realize they have been sold something they would have been better off without.

Am I saying you shouldn't invest in replacement windows and doors? No, I'm saying you should be well educated on the subject before making a buying decision. Sitting down at your kitchen table with a salesperson for two hours is rarely the best situation for making a wise decision, but this is the way many homeowners buy energy-saving windows and doors.

## CUTTING THROUGH THE HYPE

If you know the right questions to ask cutting through the hype is easy. Everyone has heard the jokes about used-car salespeople, and some people feel that home-improvement salespeople are even worse.

The home-improvement industry is plagued by horror stories of how innocent homeowners have been swindled out of their money. Unfortunately, many of these stories are true. But that doesn't mean that all home-improvement contractors are crooks.

The first step in buying replacement windows and doors is personal research. Once you know what you want, you can begin your search for a reputable contractor. If you take your time and investigate all aspects of what you are doing, you can get a good deal on products that will improve your home's energy efficiency and resale potential.

### Starting the Research

Researching the problem is as easy as calling your utility company. Most utility companies are willing to come to your house to perform an energy audit. They will do a heat-gain/heat-loss evaluation of your present windows and doors, often at no charge. This report will show you how efficient or inefficient your existing windows and doors are. You may be surprised to find that you will not benefit greatly from replacing your existing materials. If this is the case, you saved yourself thousands of dollars.

When your old windows and doors don't do well on their performance test, you may be able to find out from the utility company what your best course of action is. Something as simple as recaulking and adding weatherstripping may solve your energy problems. If your old units are beyond help, at least you will know that there will be some financial benefit to replacing them.

Some home-improvement companies offer free energy audits, but these services may be little more than an excuse to get a salesperson into your home. The utility company has nothing to gain by advising you to replace your windows and doors, but a home-improvement contractor does.

### Sifting Through the Sashes

There are so many types of windows available that sifting through the sashes can take a while. Don't call contractors to show you their samples immediately. Begin your search for the right windows by contacting suppliers and manufacturers or picking up brochures at your local lumberyard. Every major window company has detailed information available on the products available. These brochures are usually free, and they are packed with interesting information.

By studying the various brochures offered by manufacturers, you will gain familiarity with the terms and phrases used in the industry. This increase in your vocabulary will help you in talking with suppliers and contractors. Not only will it make what you are told easier to understand, your knowledge will show the vendors that you are an educated consumer.

Once you know what kind of windows and doors you want, you are ready to talk with contractors. Make a pact with yourself not to make any on-the-spot decisions. No matter how good a deal sounds, sleep on it. This will help protect you from skillful sales professionals.

### Make a Commitment

By the time you are ready to make a commitment, you should be well informed and able to make a wise buying decision. If you don't have a clear understanding of what you are doing, drop back and do more research. Replacement windows and doors can be good home improvements, but only if you get what you need at a price that is fair. There are so many ways to spend money foolishly on windows and doors that you must dedicate yourself to learning before you leap.

## WHAT TO LOOK FOR IN REPLACEMENT WINDOWS

What features should you look for in replacement windows? If you take my advice and peruse a number of brochures from various manufacturers, you will see the many options available. One thing you will always be interested in is the insulating value of the window (Figure 8-1).

| Glazings | "U" Value | "R" Value | UV Blockage | Shading Coefficient |
|---|---|---|---|---|
| **Tempered, Clear** Glazing Code 48 | 0.53 | 1.89 | 35% | 0.87 |

This unit consists of clear tempered glass, which is significantly stronger than annealed glass. It is glazed with two panes of glass, as are all VELUX Roof Windows and Skylights. We also insulate and dual-seal every unit for energy efficiency in our state-of-the-art glass plant.

| | | | | |
|---|---|---|---|---|
| **Tempered, Low-E Argon Gas-Filled** Glazing Code 75 | 0.28 | 3.57 | 60% | 0.73 |

This unit has an exterior pane of clear tempered glass with an interior pane of Low-E coated tempered glass. The Low-E coating will help retain heat in the winter, reduce heat gain in the summer and also reduce ultraviolet ray transmission. We also inject clear odorless argon gas between the panes to further improve the unit's energy efficiency.

| | | | | |
|---|---|---|---|---|
| **Tempered, Low-E Argon Gas-Filled, Bronze Tint** Glazing Code 77 | 0.28 | 3.57 | 65% | 0.57 |

This unit combines Low-E coated glass with bronze tint tempered glass to reduce heat gain year-round and also reduce ultraviolet ray transmission.

| | | | | |
|---|---|---|---|---|
| **Tempered over Laminated, Low-E Argon Gas-Filled** Glazing Code 74 | 0.32 | 3.13 | 99.9% | 0.65 |

This unit combines tempered Low-E coated glass with laminated glass to afford you all the energy efficiency of Low-E coatings in areas that require laminated glass.

| | | | | |
|---|---|---|---|---|
| **Tempered over Laminated, Low-E Argon Gas-Filled, Bronze Tint** Glazing Code 79 | 0.32 | 3.13 | 99.9% | 0.47 |

This unit combines tempered bronze tint glass with laminated glass giving you the benefits of bronze tint coating in areas that require laminated glass.

**"U" VALUE** – The total heat flow through the entire glazing assembly from room air to outside air. Lower values indicate greater insulating capability.

**"R" VALUE** – The resistance a material has to heat flow. Higher numbers indicate greater insulation capability.

**UV Blockage** – The reduction of ultraviolet ray transmission. These values are approximate as supplied by glazing manufacturer

**Shading Coefficient** – A measure of heat gain through glass from solar radiation. Specifically, the shading coefficient is the ratio between the solar heat gain from a particular type of glass and that of double strength glass. The lower the shading coefficient, the lower the solar heat gain.

Note: "R" and "U" values shown are for units as supplied by Lawrence Berkeley Laboratory, Window and Daylight Group, Window 4.0.

Figure 8-1. *Important qualities to look for in windows. Courtesy of Velux-America, Inc.*

Most people have some basic understanding of R-values for common types of insulation. They know that the larger the R-value, the better the insulating quality of the material. When you are shopping for windows, you must reverse this thought pattern. First of all, you will be dealing with U-values, not R-values. Second, the *lower* the U-value is, the better the insulating qualities of the window are.

Many people lean toward windows that are *clad* to eliminate the need for painting. If you buy unclad wood windows, you will have to paint the windows from time to time. Wood windows are normally more expensive than metal ones, but they often block more noise and do a slightly better job of insulating your home. Metal windows tend to produce condensation, and the condensation can cause damage to any wood adjacent to the window.

You will also have options for removable grids, tilting sashes, gas-filled thermal windows, solid vinyl windows, vinyl-clad windows, metal-clad windows, and others.

## HOW MUCH WILL REPLACEMENT WINDOWS COST?

The cost of replacement windows can cover a broad spectrum. If you are looking at the cost on an individual basis, you might find $150 per window to be a fair price. But many brands and styles (Figure 8-2) of windows cost more. For example, a metal-clad, double-hung wood window with dimensions of 3' X 5' might cost $185. If you want snap-in grids for this window, the price could go up $15. If you want a casement window with dimensions of 2' X 3' and the same basic specifications, the cost, without grids, might be $250. By purchasing the casement window, you are getting a smaller window and paying $65 more for it.

A plastic-clad, double-hung wood window with dimensions of 3' X 4' could set you back over $250, while a plain wood window with dimensions of 2' X 3' might cost $130. It is possible to spend much more on windows, depending on the quality and options you are interested in. There is plenty of diversity in the price of windows and their accessories.

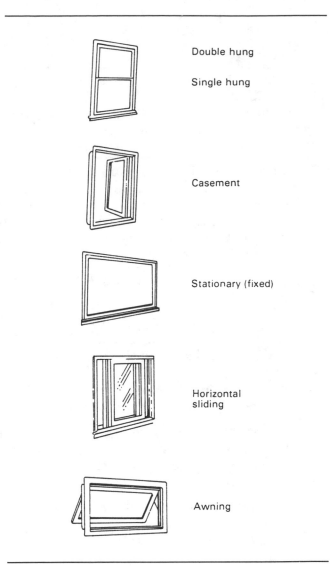

Figure 8-2. *Styles of windows. Courtesy of U.S. Dept. of Agriculture.*

### Do-it-Yourself or Not?

It is possible for homeowners to replace their own windows, but to obtain a good-looking job it is often better to hire professionals. Various techniques can be employed in replacing windows, but the method that produces the best results requires the removal of some of the home's siding. This procedure can become complicated, and homeowners can cause considerable damage to their siding if they are not competent at the task.

How much does it cost to hire professionals to replace your windows? The answer to this question depends upon how many windows will be replaced.

Let's look at an example of what it would cost to have the windows replaced in an average home.

Assume the house has a total of fourteen windows. Further assume that all the windows will be replaced with vinyl-clad aluminum windows with double panes. The size of the windows is 3' X 5'. The cost of this job, if done by professionals, will probably be between $6,000 and $6,500.

## HOW MUCH ARE REPLACEMENT WINDOWS WORTH?

What value can you expect from replacement windows? Statistics indicate that replacement windows return between 40 and 100 percent of their initial cost. Overall averages for the return run in the range of 70 percent.

When you consider that you have a good chance of recovering 70 percent of your cash investment if you sell your home, replacement windows are an average-to-good improvement. But the direct return is not the only way you get your money back.

### Energy Savings

The purpose for most replacement windows is the reduction of heating and cooling costs. If you are going to live in your home for several years after the windows are replaced, you should save money on your utility bills. How much money will you save on your home heating and cooling costs? The heat-gain/heat-loss report you obtained from your utility company should provide the answer to this question.

You might find that your old windows account for 20 percent of your heat loss. By working with your utility company and window supplier, you should be able to determine how much new windows will reduce your heat loss, and what the reduction will amount to in fuel dollars.

Let's assume your annual heating and cooling costs run $1,200. For the sake of our example, let's say that your old windows account for $200 of this expense. If you find that the new windows will cut your heat loss from the windows in half, the new windows will save you $100 per year. Your circumstances could result in much higher savings, but they could also represent lower savings. This example is only meant to show you how to calculate the pay-back on your new windows.

Let's say you spent $6,000 on replacement windows that will save you $100 a year; it is going to take sixty years to recover your investment! Obviously, this is not a very cost-effective improvement, under these conditions.

Suppose you stay in your home for seven years and then sell it, how much money will you lose? If you realize a 70 percent return on your initial investment, you will recover $4,200 from the cost of your windows when the house is sold. You will also have saved $100 a year for seven years. The total recovery from the windows is $4,900, so you lost $1,100.

If this were a real evaluation, it would be difficult to justify the new windows. While you would be a good citizen for conserving energy, you would be losing money. Since the windows are not likely to provide any particular personal enjoyment, the loss of $1,100 would be hard to swallow.

While the real numbers for your home will be different, you can use this type of logic and formula to calculate the value of replacement windows for your home.

There will, of course, be times when the savings on the cost of utilities will be much greater than the example used above. If your home has old, drafty windows, the savings could amount to several hundred dollars a year. Under these circumstances, the improvement becomes very viable. The numbers used in the example were kept at conservative levels to prove the point that replacement windows are not always the great deal they appear to be.

## REPLACEMENT DOORS

Replacement doors are often installed along with replacement windows. Unlike windows, doors are relatively easy to replace, and almost any homeowner can accomplish the task. You might replace your front door to improve the appearance of your home. Added security could be another reason for wanting to replace your existing door and, of course, energy savings could be your motivation.

Whatever your reason for replacing a main entry door, you will have an abundant source of doors from which to choose. The prices for exterior doors start around $100 and go up, sometimes way up. A budget of $250 will allow you a wide selection of both steel-insulated doors and wood doors. An investment of this sort is not going to break your bank account, but it can dress up your house and save you some money on your heating and cooling costs.

If you are thinking of spending $1,000 for a front door, think long and hard. For most houses, justifying such an expense is not possible.

Will the replacement of your entry doors increase your home's value? Probably not, but it may make the house more attractive and energy efficient. Considering the modest costs involved, replacement doors can make good weekend projects.

The value of replacement doors and windows depends largely on individual circumstances. This chapter has given you enough information to allow you to assess your personal situation. Research is a key ingredient to making any wise buying decision, but when it comes to replacement windows, research is critical. If you don't want to spend the next sixty years recovering money invested in replacement windows, do the research, do the math, and know what you want before you sign a contract to have the work done.

Now let's move on to Chapter 9 and see if you should build that fireplace you have always wanted.

# FIREPLACES AND WOOD STOVES 9

Fireplaces and wood stoves are improvements that can add warmth and atmosphere to a home. There is something about the smell of wood smoke and the flickering of gentle flames that is soothing. If you have ever backed up to a warm wood stove on a cold day, you know there is no other feeling quite like it. Without question, a fireplace or wood stove can add a new dimension to a house.

Fireplaces are not a standard feature in most modern homes. The costs involved with building a fireplace can put the price of a home out of reach for some buyers. Since fireplaces are not efficient heat sources and their main benefit is their charm, builders began putting fireplaces on option lists rather than in family rooms.

Many homeowners would love to have a beautiful brick hearth to settle down next to on a cold winter night, but because most houses don't have fireplaces, these homeowners can only fantasize about hanging stockings from the mantel at Christmas or sipping hot tea while watching golden flames dance before their eyes.

If you are one of those homeowners who would like a fireplace but feel it's not practical to have one added to your house, you might be surprised with what you will learn from this chapter.

Wood stoves became very popular some years back, when heating costs skyrocketed. Wood-burning stoves have long played an important role in the home. They have been used for cooking and heating for years and years. While wood cook-stoves are no longer common, it is still easy to find wood stoves in use for heating homes.

Wood stoves are found in basements, family rooms, country kitchens, and even living rooms. Their designs and finishes can complement the most formal rooms in a home, and their ability to produce quick, hot heat is legendary. There are wood stoves with glass fronts, screen doors, designer colors, engraved exteriors, and more.

Wood stoves of airtight design can maintain a warm fire for hours, without attention. It is possible to fill the firebox before going to bed and wake up to a warm house, with a fire still burning in the stove. With this type of stove there is no need to get up in the middle of the night to feed wood to the fire.

Accessories for both fireplaces and wood stoves are available to improve heating efficiency and even to heat water. Coiled piping can allow the fire to heat water, and blowers can disperse the radiant heat given off from fireplaces and stoves.

When you consider that either of these improvements can provide supplemental heat, charm, and increased resale potential for your home, it is no wonder they are popular.

## INSTALLING WOOD STOVES

Installing a wood stove is not a complicated chore, if you have a flue available for connecting the stove pipe. When there is an existing flue in serviceable condition, connecting a wood stove is simple. All that is required is running a pipe from the top (or back) of the stove to the thimble in the flue and cementing the pipe in place.

Local fire codes may have rules governing the exact installation of a stove, but the procedure is easy, as long as you have a flue to connect to. But what can you do if you don't have a flue? There are two basic options: you can have a masonry flue built, or you can use multi-wall stovepipe to create your own flue.

Building a masonry flue (Figure 9-1) can cost a couple thousand dollars or more, but multi-wall pipe can be used to construct a suitable flue for a fraction of that cost. Flues made from double- and triple-wall pipe are common, and they can be run inside the home or along an outside wall. Special mounting kits are available for piping that penetrates ceilings and walls.

Due to the design of multi-wall pipe, it can be placed in close proximity to drywall. This allows a metal pipe installed inside the home to be con-

cealed in a chase that is covered with drywall. It is also acceptable, and often attractive, to leave the stovepipe exposed.

## WHAT WILL IT COST TO INSTALL A METAL FLUE?

What costs should you expect for installation of a metal flue? The cost depends on the method of installation and the location of the stove, in relation to the home's roof. Let's look at two examples of installing a metal flue: one on the inside of the home, and one on the outside of the home.

### An Interior Flue

An interior flue is simple to install when you use multi-wall stovepipe. Before you install any type of flue, check your local fire and building codes for regulations and permit requirements. Even if you will be hiring a contractor to do the work for you, it is wise to check local regulations yourself (Figure 9-2). Some contractors may try to cut their costs by avoiding required permits and inspections, so your research could pay off in the form of a safer job.

For our cost example, let's assume you own a one-story house and want to install a wood stove in the family room. The stove will be installed near one of the corners of the room and the stovepipe will be left exposed to accentuate the rustic look of the room.

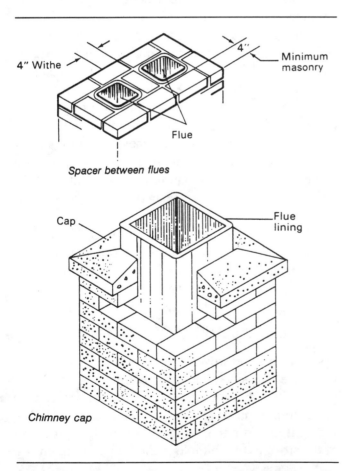

Figure 9-1. *Masonry flue. Courtesy of U.S. Dept. of Agriculture.*

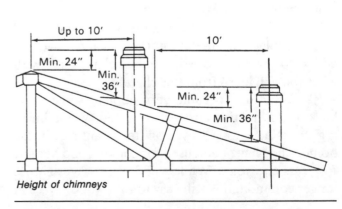

Figure 9-2. *Common code requirements for chimney heights. Courtesy of U.S. Dept. of Agriculture.*

To start with, you will need a ceiling support, a stove pipe adapter, and a chimney cap. All of these items can be purchased in a kit for less than $120. You will need enough multi-wall pipe and connectors to get up through the attic and to extend at least a few feet above the roof penetration. This should cost about $210. The last item you will need is an approved roof collar; it should cost around $10. Your total cost for materials is $350, and installation is simple.

### An Exterior Flue

Let's assume about the same circumstances as in the example above, except this time we will run the stove pipe out the exterior wall and up the side of the house.

You can buy a kit that contains a wall support, wall thimble, and tee fitting with cleanout, stove-pipe adapter, and other miscellaneous items needed for about $250. You may still need a roof collar, at a cost of $10, and pipe at a cost of $210. The total cost for the job done this way is $470, and installation is still easy.

It is simple to see why multi-wall metal flues are used much more often than masonry flues; metal flues cost considerably less.

According to the appraiser I interviewed for this book, the installation of a metal flue will almost always pay for itself in resale value, if the job is done in a professional manner and if the house is of a style where a wood stove may be desirable. Most professionals and statistics agree that installing a metal flue is a low-risk improvement, financially.

## WOOD STOVE PRICES

Wood stove prices have a wide range. You can buy small stoves for around $300, but most units have prices closer to $500. Big stoves and stoves with special features can cross over the $1,000 mark. When blowers are added to the cost of a stove, expect an increase of about $125.

If you decide to sell your house, you can take your stove with you. Wood stoves are considered personal property and are not required to convey with the sale of real estate. If you plan to keep your stove when your house is sold, make sure potential buyers are aware of your intentions.

## MASONRY FIREPLACES

Masonry fireplaces are a favorite amenity in many homes. If your home doesn't have a fireplace, adding one could be a good investment and an enjoyable experience.

The cost of having a masonry fireplace built will be much more than installing a wood stove, and the heating efficiency will not be as good, but the end result can still be very desirable.

Unless you have unusual talents for an average homeowner, this is a job for professionals. Building a masonry fireplace is hard work, and the process is tricky.

### How Much Will a Masonry Fireplace Cost?

How much will a masonry fireplace (Figure 9-3) cost? To establish a cost, let's assume the fireplace will be cut into an outside gable wall of your family room. A foundation will be needed, and the chimney will terminate about twenty feet above the ground. The job's cost will include a standard masonry hearth and a heavy mantel.

The materials for this job will cost about $1,250. But since most homeowners can't do the job themselves, a cost for labor must be considered. Depending upon where you live and what the economy is like, you might find a mason to build the fireplace for as little as $2,500, but the labor could cost as much as $3,500. The total cost for materials and labor should fall somewhere between $3,500 and $4,500.

If you relocate the fireplace to a wall without a gable end, you can reduce the cost considerably. The chimney will not have to extend as high, and the cost of labor and materials will go down.

If we pick an average cost of $4,000, how much of the money can be recovered if you sell your home? Most professionals agree that you have a good chance of recovering all of your investment.

## FREE-STANDING FIREPLACES

Free-standing fireplaces are not as popular as more traditional fireplaces, but they are much less expensive. The chimney for a free-standing fireplace can be made in the same way as described for wood stoves. Free-standing fireplaces are often priced well below $1,000 and do provide an affordable alternative to more expensive fireplace options.

As for resale value, the free-standing fireplace will not be as likely to produce a full return on your investment, but if you install it yourself, you should not lose any money.

## BUILT-IN PRE-FAB FIREPLACES

Built-in pre-fab fireplaces provide a project most homeowners can do themselves that will be cost effective and provide a more traditional style of fireplace.

The chimneys for these types of fireplaces can be made with the same multi-wall pipe used for wood stoves. Once the fireplace unit is set in place and the chimney is installed, a box can be built to conceal the firebox and chimney. This built-in look simulates the appearance of a masonry fireplace. A brick facade can be added to enhance the illusion.

The cost of materials for everything needed to make a first-class imitation of a masonry fireplace will cost about $1,500. If you are not concerned with a brick facing, false-brick chimney cap, and other assorted decorative items, you can buy the materials needed for a fine-looking fireplace for about $1,100. This is such a bargain any handy homeowner can take advantage of it.

If you are not the hands-on type, you can hire contractors to do the job for you. The cost for these services will probably run between $1,200 and $1,500. Even if you pay for a premium job, you will have no more than $3,000 invested.

Personally, if I were going to pay $3,000 for a pre-fab installation, I would stretch my budget and find a way to get a masonry fireplace. While pre-fab units are functional and desirable, they don't carry the clout of a masonry fireplace in terms of looks or resale value.

Installing your own pre-fab fireplace is a safe bet financially. Paying full retail price for the job may put you on weaker ground when it comes time to recover your investment.

### Decorative Fireplaces

Most decorative fireplaces run from $300 to $500. By the time you add electric logs and a mantel, the cost is pushed up by about $150. Some people like these artificial units, but I can't see spending $650 for a fake fireplace when I could build in a pre-fab unit for $1,100. I suppose if you want the look of a fireplace without the hassle of wood and ashes, the decorative units make sense, but I like to smell the fire and feel the heat.

Since decorative fireplaces are personal property, they will probably not add any value to your home. They may, however, help to make your home more appealing to prospective buyers. Now, let's move on to the next chapter and check out walls, ceilings, and insulation.

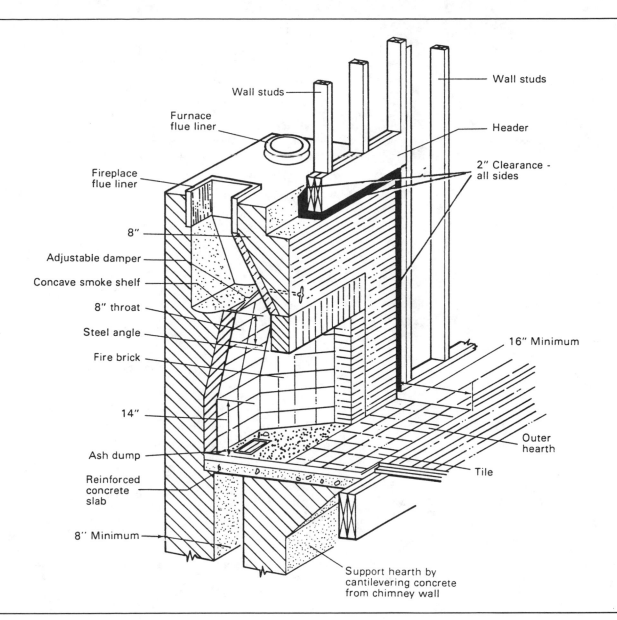

Figure 9-3. *Masonry fireplace. Courtesy of U.S. Dept. of Agriculture.*

# WALLS, CEILINGS, AND INSULATION

A home's walls, ceilings, and insulation sometimes require attention. Work done on these parts of a home is often considered maintenance, but there are also times when the work is a planned improvement. This chapter is going to look at many aspects of working with your walls, ceilings, and insulation.

Have you been wondering what it would cost to install ceramic tile on your bathroom floor? Is this the year you are planning to upgrade the insulation in your home? Have you tired of looking at the same old ceilings? There are numerous ways and reasons to improve the interior of your home, and we are going to look at the most popular ones in this chapter. Let's start with insulation upgrades.

## Upgrading Your Insulation

Upgrading your insulation can reduce your heating and cooling costs, but will the cost of the project be a worthwhile investment? If you don't have the answer yet, don't worry, you are about to find out.

Before deciding to upgrade your insulation, you should verify the amount of insulation you currently have. It also helps to know how much insulation should be in various parts of your home. The U.S. Department of Energy's Technical Information Center can provide you with information that will allow you to determine how much insulation your home should have. They can be reached at:

U.S. Department of Energy
Technical Information Center
P.O. Box 62
Oak Ridge, TN 37830

To give you an idea of what to expect, let me give you some examples for different parts of the country. If you live in Maine, you should have heavy insulation. The exterior walls of your home should contain enough insulation to provide a rating of R-11, although many builders in Maine install enough insulation to bring the rating up to R-19. If the house has a crawlspace, the floor joists of the first floor should hold insulation with a rating of R-19. Attic insulation for homes in Maine should be rated at R-49.

If you live in Florida, you can get by with less insulation. The attic should be rated at R-19, the exterior-wall insulation should be R-11, and the crawlspace should not require any insulation.

Homes through much of the Midwest should have the areas of their homes insulated as follows: attic—R-38, exterior walls—R-11, crawlspace joists —R-19.

Minimum recommendations for insulation in exterior walls and crawlspace areas are pretty consistent across the county, but attic insulation can vary from R-19 to R-49, depending on the climate.

To verify the R-value of your present insulation, you will have to gain access to it. This is usually simple in attics and crawlspaces, but exterior walls are more difficult to check. One way to check the amount and type of insulation contained in an outside wall is to remove the coverplate of an electrical outlet and investigate the wall's contents. If you do this, be careful not to come into contact with electrical wiring that may shock you.

Once you have found and measured your existing

insulation, you will need to convert the information you have gained to an R-value. Different types of insulation carry different R-value ratings. Here are some examples of different types of common insulation and their R-values.

| Insulation Type | R-Value | Comments |
|---|---|---|
| Vermiculite | 2.2 per inch | |
| Fiberglass | 3.5 per inch | Most common type |
| Polystyrene | 3.5 per inch | |
| Rock wool | 3.5 per inch | |
| Cellulose | 3.6 per inch | |
| Urethane foam | 5.5 per inch | Flammable, can emit cyanide gas if ignited, not legal in all areas |

Now you know how much insulation you should have, and you know how to convert the depth of insulation in your home to R-values. Once you have measured and rated your present insulation, deciding on the value of additional insulation should be easy. If your present insulation is below recommended standards, you should add more insulation. If the existing insulation in your home meets recommended R-values, adding more insulation probably is not worthwhile.

### How Much Will It Cost to Upgrade My Home's Insulation?

How much should you expect to pay to upgrade your home's insulation? The cost to upgrade your insulation will depend on the type of insulation used, how it is installed, and whether you will do the work yourself. Almost anyone can install most forms of insulation, but some people have allergic reactions to certain types of insulation materials.

To arrive at cost figures, let's assume the house we are working with is a one-level home with a crawlspace. The dimensions of the house are 24' X 44'. Insulation in the crawlspace is nonexistent, and the attic has fiberglass insulation with an R-value of R-19. You want to install enough insulation to get an R-value of R-19 in the crawlspace and R-38 in the attic. You have decided to use batts of fiberglass insulation, and you will do the work yourself.

Both the attic and the crawlspace have a total area of 1,056 square feet of space to be insulated. You will be installing a complete layer of R-19 insu-

lation in both locations to achieve your goal, so you need 2,112 square feet of R-19 insulation. You will also need some wire hangers to hold the crawlspace insulation in place.

The hangers will cost less than $10. Where and when you buy your insulation will have some bearing on its price, but you should be safe in assuming a square-foot cost of $0.45. The total cost of materials for this job is about $960.

I just recently saw faced fiberglass insulation with an R-value of R-30 advertised for only $0.36 per square foot. If you shop around for your insulation, you might get the cost of this job down to $700.

### Will it Pay for Itself?

Now that you've spent $950 for insulation, how long will it take for the insulation to pay for itself? The most accurate way to determine your payback period is to work with your utility company and obtain a heat-gain/heat-loss report. If your present insulation is nonexistent or far below recommended levels, your investment could pay for itself very quickly. However, if you are just adding insulation to an already ample amount, the payback period could stretch out into decades.

When an upgrade in insulation is warranted, it can pay for itself in as little as three years, but five to seven years would be a safer guess. If you pile on insulation unnecessarily, it might take twenty-five years to recover your costs.

## WALLCOVERINGS

Wallcoverings are a type of improvement that many homeowners can do themselves. Whether it is painting or papering, anyone with average skills can produce a job that looks good. Ceramic tile is even within the capability range of most homeowners.

Many older homes have walls that have become dull and lifeless over their years of use. When walls become boring, many homeowners elect to pump new life into them with fresh wallcoverings. Are wallcoverings a good way to spend the money you have set aside for home improvements? Well, let's take a close look at the various types of wallcoverings, one at a time, and see.

## Paint

Painting is a fast way to change the way your interior walls look. If the walls are in good repair, painting is easy and effective. While painting will do little to increase the value of your home in terms of dollars, it can make a dramatic difference in the appearance your home presents. Painting walls a new color can even change your mental attitude.

The cost of painting an average room is minimal. Let's assume you want to paint your living room and that the room dimensions are 16' X 22'. Based on the assumption that the walls are a standard height, you will have approximately 600 square feet of wall surface to paint. If the walls are in good shape and do not need anything more than two coats of fresh paint, the materials for your project can be bought for less than $40. If a top-of-the-line paint is desired, the cost might be $75. In either case, the cost of materials doesn't amount to much. Allow for extra expense if you plan to paint the trim or ceiling.

Painting this room is going to do very little for the appraised value of your home, but it is an inexpensive project that can enhance your habitat's appearance.

## Wallpaper

Have you thought of hanging wallpaper in your bathroom? Unlike painting, adding wallpaper in your home can increase the property's value. The increase in value won't be a lot, but it will be more than a fresh coat of paint will return.

Hanging wallpaper requires patience and planning, but it is a job most homeowners can handle. As for cost, wallpaper is more expensive than paint, but it is still a bargain if you hang it yourself. Let's look at the cost to install wallpaper in an average bathroom.

The bathroom we are working with is 5' X 8' and has a window and a tub-shower combination. The tub-shower combination covers most of one wall, and the door and window take up some of the wall space. In round numbers, there are about 150 square feet of wall to cover with paper. To allow for waste and lining up patterns, we will estimate a need for 175 square feet.

Wallpaper comes in different sizes and rolls contain various quantities of paper, but the paper we are using contains about 56 square feet per roll, at a cost of $25 per roll. If everything goes as planned, we should be able to get by with three rolls, but since mistakes can be made, we are going to buy four rolls to be safe. The cost for the paper is $100. By the time we buy adhesive and a few miscellaneous items, we may have $125 invested.

Spending $125 and a few hours to paper your bathroom is a very wise move. The wallpaper will make the bathroom more elegant, and it will evoke a feeling of higher value in your home. Some if not all of your investment will be recovered in appraised value, and if you decide to sell your home, buyers will be impressed with the new wallcovering.

If you don't want to wallpaper the walls of a room, but want to add an accent, you can use decorative strips of wallpaper. These strips can be used as borders where the walls meet the ceilings, or they can be used at a mid-point on the walls to define the theme of a room (Figure 10-1).

## Ceramic Tile

Ceramic tile is another way to add extra value to areas of your home. While a professionally-installed tile job may be cost prohibitive, doing the job yourself is not only possible, it can be profitable.

Tile works best on the walls of a bathroom or kitchen (Figure 10-2). You could install tile between the top of your counter and the bottom of your cabinets in the kitchen. Running tile halfway up the bathroom wall can give the room a more distinguished look. Combining tile and wallpaper in a bathroom can produce fantastic results.

The walls surrounding your bathtub are another place ceramic tile will fit in nicely. A tiled tub surround is considered an upgrade over plastic or fiberglass surrounds.

Should you choose to install tile on any of your walls, the hardest part of the job may be picking the perfect tile. There are so many shapes, colors, and patterns available to choose from that it could boggle your mind.

Like wallpaper, ceramic tile requires patience and planning for a professional look. You will want to have the tiles spaced evenly, and only proper measuring and planning will allow this. Setting wall tile is not difficult, but you should dedicate some time to researching installation methods before you attempt this job.

### How Much Will a Tiled Tub Surround Cost?

How much will you spend for a tiled tub surround? Here in Maine, I can hire a professional tile contractor to supply and install the materials to surround a standard bathtub for just under $400, and the quality of materials and workmanship is excellent.

If you do the job yourself, you will need to either rent or buy a tile cutter. For a standard tub surround, you will need about 50 square feet of tile. Depending upon the type and quality of tile you select, you can expect to pay between $1.00 and $2.00 per square foot for average materials. At the most, your tub tiles shouldn't cost more than $100. You will also need some adhesive and grouting materials, but these items don't cost much. If you budget $175 for your materials and tool rental, you should be fine. Can you imagine having a tiled tub surround for less than the cost of many plastic glue-on walls?

By doing the work yourself, you almost guarantee an equity gain in your home. It can't compare with the equity you could earn by building a room addition, but on a percentage basis, it will be a strong return on your cash investment. Your tiled tub surround will be worth $365 to $500.

## WAINSCOTING

Adding wainscoting and decorative trim to a dining room transforms the room from average to formal. It also increases the value of the room. Living rooms and family rooms can also benefit from wainscoting.

Even if you possess only the most basic carpentry skills, you can install your own wainscoting. You can use sheets of paneling for the job, or you can install tongue-and-groove boards. The top of the wainscoting will need to be trimmed with a chair rail, but even this part of the job is not very difficult.

If you are installing wainscoting on a wall already finished with drywall, you may want to cut out and remove the drywall where the wainscoting will be installed. This is a necessity if you are using a thick wood for your wainscoting. If you are using a thin paneling, you can install it right over the existing drywall.

### How Much Will It Cost to Add Wainscoting?

How much will adding wainscoting to your dining room cost? The cost depends on the type of material used. Let's assume the room dimensions are 12' X 12'. This will give you a wall area of 192 feet to cover, less any space occupied by doors or cased openings.

Paneling is usually sold in 4' X 8' sheets. Since wainscoting usually extends four feet up a wall, this works out very nicely. You will need six sheets of paneling to cover the walls with standard wainscoting. Paneling can be bought for as little as $5.00 a sheet, but the good stuff will cost closer to $20. Using a good quality paneling, the cost of materials will be $120. In addition to this cost, you will need 48 feet, less the amount not used in doorways, for the top trim. Trim wood is expensive, and depending on what you choose to use, the trim could cost as much as the paneling, or more.

A small amount of stain or paint will be needed for the trim, but it won't cost much. If you are willing to spend $250, you can add wainscoting to a dining room of this size. Should you decide to use more elaborate materials, the cost might double.

Using individual boards for the wainscoting could put the price at more than $1,000. While there are times when the more expensive routes are justified, you are less likely to recover your investment when you opt for the most expensive wainscoting. Sticking with materials that cost around $300 is a pretty safe bet, but spending $1,000 on materials will more than likely result in a loss.

Professional trim carpenters are expensive. Turning to professionals to install your wainscoting can destroy its equity-building potential.

## PANELING

Installing paneling on the walls in your family room can be a good idea, but this project will not usually pay for itself. In most cases, paneled walls are not worth more than painted walls, but they are more expensive.

If you decide to install paneling, be careful not to choose wood tones that will darken the room. Installing dark paneling is a mistake many homeowners make, and a dark room is not only dreary to live in, it is hard to sell to prospective buyers. There are many shades of paneling now available in lighter tones, some even with pickled or lightly tinted finishes.

## CEILINGS

### Creativity Doesn't Necessarily Pay

People sometimes want to be creative with their ceilings. They may want to add false beams to give a room a more rustic look. Some people will want to install an acoustical ceiling, and a number of people texture their ceilings. Should you invest money in giving your ceilings a new look? If the existing ceilings are in good shape, you should limit your improvements to fresh paint.

Most appraisers and real estate brokers agree that a painted ceiling is as valuable as any other type of ceiling. While ceilings with imitation beams and wood planking can change the atmosphere of a room, they are not likely to increase the room's value. The same is true of vaulted ceilings.

From an emotional, and sometimes a sales, perspective, vaulted ceilings and exposed beams can be very beneficial. A tongue-and-groove planked ceiling can add warmth and charm to a room, but again, it is not likely to add much value. The cost involved with getting creative on ceilings is usually not recovered in the sale of a property or on an appraisal report.

### Damaged Ceilings

When existing ceilings are sagging or showing water stains, replacing or covering them is a wise investment. At these times there are many options available. The three most common methods for dealing with these types of ceiling include: acoustical ceiling tiles, new drywall and paint, and ceiling textures. Of the three, texturing is the least expensive, but it will not always solve the problem.

To examine the most cost-effective ways to improve a damaged ceiling, let's look at the three most common methods individually. In our first example, assume there has been a leak in the upstairs bathroom that has created an ugly water stain in the ceiling of the downstairs hall. The stain spreads out two feet in each direction, and you don't believe it can be hidden with a coat of primer and paint. What will you do?

Installing an acoustical ceiling is not practical. This type of ceiling would be out of place in a hallway, and it would not match the other ceilings that are visible from the hall.

If the damaged ceiling is structurally sound (the drywall is not sagging), texturing the ceiling is a reasonable and cost-effective way to correct the problem. For less than $25, you can seal the stain and texture the ceiling. This solves your problem with next to no investment.

Assuming the damaged drywall has lost its shape, you could cut out the section and replace it. If you are not an expert at taping and finishing drywall seams, you can hide your minor imperfections by texturing the ceiling after replacing the damaged portion. Under these circumstances, you will probably have to spend $45 to correct the problem. Still, you have made an economical improvement that is well worth the cost.

For another example, assume you have a family room where the existing ceiling is made from plaster and is deteriorating. Under these circumstances, texturing the ceiling will not solve the problem. If you want to install drywall, you will have your work cut out for you. Removing the plaster and lath is an enormous job in itself, and after that is done, you will have to use furring strips to level the ceiling joists. Otherwise, the drywall will have a ripple effect in it that will not be easy to hide.

The best solution to this ceiling problem is probably an acoustical ceiling. By using a ceiling that is supported by a hanging metal framework, the uneven existing ceiling will not be much of a problem to work around. For about $1.25 per square foot, you can buy the materials needed to install a good acoustical ceiling. For a family room with dimensions of 16' X 24', this amounts to $480.

In general, you will normally be better off investing your home-improvement dollars in some part of your home other than the ceilings. But when your ceilings are stained or sagging, giving them some attention is important to maintaining the value of your home.

After you are done working with your walls and ceilings, your attention might turn to your floors. If so, you're in luck; the next chapter is about flooring. We will compare the costs and values of hardwood floors, wall-to-wall carpeting, tiled floors, and more.

Figure 10-1. *This decorative wallpaper border would be great for a study or a child's room. Courtesy of Lis King Public Relations and Environmental Graphics, Inc.*

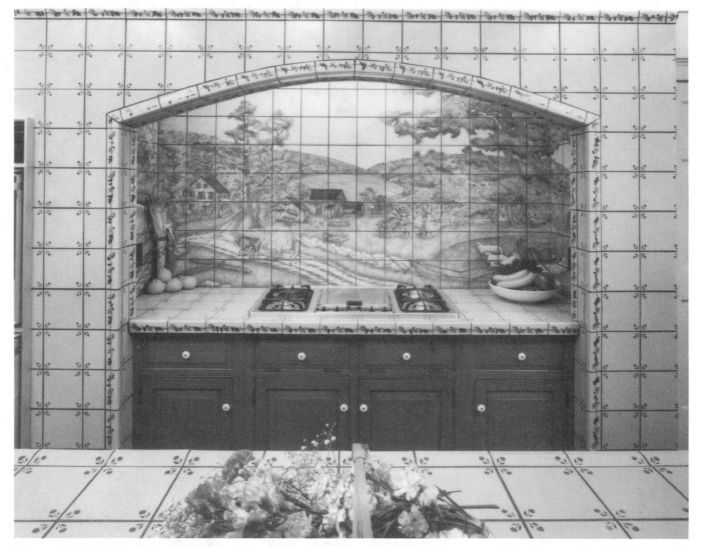

Figure 10-2. *This kitchen incorporates extensive use of decorative tile. Courtesy of Lis King Public Relations and Summitville Tiles.*

# FLOORING

Flooring is a type of home improvement that is often taken for granted. When many homeowners think of remodeling, they usually envision carpentry work and possibly plumbing, but not flooring. Yet flooring is often a part of remodeling jobs, and it can be the primary element of remodeling.

Once people start to think about flooring, they frequently become enthralled with the options available. They can become so infatuated with colors, designs, and types of floor coverings that they lose sight of their objective.

## FLOORING CAN MAKE A BIG DIFFERENCE

Replacing a dark carpet with a light carpet can make a major difference in a room. The room can instantly appear larger, brighter, and more inviting. Considering the relatively low cost of flooring as a home improvement, it should attract more attention from the consumer than it generally does.

While homeowners often replace the flooring in a room being remodeled, they rarely *just* replace the flooring. Why is this? Unless a floor has become badly worn or is an eyesore, most people simply don't think about the effect new flooring would have on the room.

Think about your home for a moment. Would installing quarry tile in the foyer make the home more impressive? It probably would, and this is a job you could do yourself without spending a lot of money. Imagine how your bathroom would look if you removed the old vinyl flooring and replaced it with ceramic tile. It would look great, wouldn't it? Would installing tile on your bathroom floor increase your home's value? It should; the increase wouldn't be astronomical, but the value and look of the room should improve with the installation of ceramic tile.

Take a look at the carpeting in your family room or living room. Does it date your home? Some types of carpet are a dead giveaway to a home's age. While much of your home's appearance may not indicate age, the carpet can stand out like a pair of bell-bottom, floral-print pants. Replacing your carpeting to give the floor of your home a face-lift may not always be cost-effective in terms of increased value, but it can improve immensely the visual impact and appeal of the house.

We talked earlier about installing wainscoting and trim to give your dining room a more formal look; can you imagine what adding hardwood flooring would do for the image? Hardwood flooring is expensive, but it should increase your home's value, and there is no doubt it will change the feel of the room.

Kitchens are another place flooring can be a big part of how the space is interpreted. If your kitchen is equipped with a dull brown sheet of vinyl flooring, maybe you should install some tile. You could go for the eye-opening look of black and white squares, or you might decide on a nice almond color. Fitting the floor with tile will transform the kitchen from a normal subdivision-type look to a custom-home kitchen. Without question, flooring can do a lot to change the look of your home.

## Investment Value

Okay, the power of flooring can be a strong influence on your home, but is flooring a good investment? Some types of flooring are better investments than others. Normally, replacing carpet with carpet is not a good move financially; however, replacing vinyl flooring in a bathroom with ceramic tile can be. Covering hardwood flooring with carpeting is generally a mistake, but replacing carpeting with hardwood flooring in certain rooms can produce a higher value for your home. The key is knowing what types of flooring changes to make and when to make them. This chapter shows you the secrets of finding the most value in floor coverings.

## CARPETING

Carpeting is by far the most widely used floor covering. Wall-to-wall carpeting is often found in every room of a modern home, with the exceptions of kitchens and bathrooms. While carpeting is an accepted industry standard, that very fact can make it mundane.

Good carpeting can last a long time, but after a while, it can discolor and lose its freshness. This is especially true if children or pets routinely pass over the carpeting. Once carpeting becomes worn and dull, it begins to detract from the appearance and value of your home. When this happens, replacement is the logical solution. However, replacing damaged or worn carpeting probably isn't going to result in a profitable investment. Don't take this the wrong way. Your house will be worth more than it would with dilapidated carpeting, but the improvement will not make the house worth much more than it would be worth if the old carpet were still serviceable.

If your house has wall-to-wall carpeting, the flooring is expected to be in good condition; if that isn't the case, the value of your home will suffer. But replacing good carpet with better carpet will not normally have much impact on an appraisal report. In terms of appraised value, carpeting is carpeting: it doesn't make much difference if the carpet cost $18 a yard or $28 a yard, it is still carpet.

High grades of carpeting can be worth a little more on an appraisal than standard carpeting, but the increased value will not offset the increased cost. This is also true of the pad installed under the carpeting. While superior padding will make carpeting last longer, look better, and feel nicer, it will not pay its way on an appraisal report.

Installing new carpeting can do wonders for the appearance and appeal of your home, but the improvement is not one of the most profitable home improvements available. If you are willing to make the investment for your personal enjoyment or for sales appeal, new carpeting is worth considering, but if you are looking to build equity or turn a profit on your investment, carpeting should be low on your priority list.

## How Much Would New Carpeting Cost?

How much would installing new carpeting cost? The cost of carpeting can vary tremendously, and so can the expense of padding and installation. Wall-to-wall carpeting can be installed by homeowners, but the job is not easy, and a mistake can be expensive. Professional installers are not cheap, but they may be a bargain. Buying carpet by the roll to do the job yourself may cost nearly as much as paying to have it installed professionally. When you consider the value of your time, the expense of renting the tools needed for a proper installation, and the risk of ruining the flooring, paying professionals to do the job for you is probably your best course of action.

To get an idea of what new carpeting costs, let's create a sample room and replace the carpeting in it. What would it cost to replace the carpeting in a family room with dimensions of 16' X 24'? The first expense is the removal of the existing carpeting and pad. This is a job any average homeowner can do, but if you have the removal included in the total price for a professional job, the cost will run at least $1.25 per square yard.

To determine square yardage, you take the square footage of a room and divide it by nine. The family room we are examining has 384 square feet of flooring area. This translates into 42.67 square yards, so we will just call it 43 square yards. At $1.25 per square yard, the cost for having the old carpeting and pad removed is under $60.

Like any other job, the prices in different areas vary. While I can have a professional remove carpeting and pad for $1.25 per square yard, the work in your area may cost twice that much. You should also ask if the fee for removing the old materials includes disposing of them. Many installers price the job based on removing the old flooring from the floor, not from your property.

With the old flooring out of the way, what is it going to cost to have new carpeting professionally installed? This is where prices can fluctuate greatly. As a contractor, I can have a professional supply and install name-brand pad and carpeting that will meet government housing standards for about $13 per square yard, if I'm having carpet installed throughout a new house. On a small job, my cost is around $15 a yard. With this being the case, I could carpet the family room for about $650.

As a homeowner, you will normally pay a bit more than a professional remodeling contractor would for carpeting. Your cost for this same job, using the same flooring company and materials, might run $750.

If we choose to put more than a basic builder-grade carpeting in the room, the cost could double. If you want top-of-the-line padding and carpeting, a price of $30 a yard should not shock you. In most cases, buying as a homeowner, a budget of $23 a yard should buy a better-than-average grade of carpeting, installed. Figuring a total cost of $25 per square yard should take care of removing the old flooring and having new pad and carpet installed. At $25 a yard, the cost to install new carpet in the sample family room would be $1,075.

How much of your $1,075 will you get back if you sell your home? You probably won't see much of a return on your investment for the reasons discussed above, but the improvement may be a factor in selling your house faster.

## SHEET-VINYL FLOORING

Sheet-vinyl flooring can be compared to carpeting when evaluating the return on your investment. Replacing vinyl with vinyl isn't likely to increase your home's value. But some forms of high-grade flooring (Figure 11-1) can increase the perceived and real value of a home. For example, installing an attractive, high-quality vinyl in a foyer can produce excellent results (Figure 11-2).

This type of flooring is common in bathrooms and kitchens. Since bathrooms and kitchens are two of the most important rooms in homes in terms of sales value, it makes sense to have attractive flooring in them. But this doesn't mean the money you spend on new vinyl flooring will come back to you at the time of a sale; in all probability, it won't.

## How Much Does it Cost to Install New Vinyl Flooring?

How much does installation of new vinyl flooring cost? Like carpeting, there are many different grades of vinyl flooring, and price depends on the type and quality of flooring chosen. The condition of an existing subfloor can also influence the overall cost of installing new vinyl. If the subfloor is not in good condition, underlayment may need to be installed, and this runs up the total cost of the job, sometimes considerably.

New vinyl flooring can be installed over existing vinyl, but most professionals don't recommend this practice. Normally, the old flooring is removed and the subfloor is prepared to accept new flooring. What type of preparation is needed? Sometimes no special preparation is required, but it is not unusual to have to fill cracks and depressions with filler material. If a subfloor is in bad condition, underlayment might be installed over the subfloor, to create a clean, flat, smooth surface for the new vinyl.

To visualize the cost of replacing the vinyl flooring in your kitchen, let's work through an example of the job. Assume your kitchen's dimensions are 10' X 12'. This is 120 square feet, or just under 14 square yards.

A builder-grade vinyl professionally installed in one room will cost a homeowner about $18 a yard. This is assuming the existing subfloor does not require any special preparation and that the old flooring has been removed. The per-square-yard cost translates into a total cost of $250.

The odds of not having to pay for any preparation work are against you; most subfloors require some preparation. If minimal prep work is required, the cost will go up by about $50. If underlayment has to be installed, expect a price increase of at least $125.

Figure 11-1. *High-quality vinyl flooring in this kitchen adds value, good looks, and easy care. Courtesy of Azrock Industries, Azrock Floor Products.*

Figure 11-2. *The high-quality vinyl flooring in this foyer gives the effect of a much more expensive flooring. Photo courtesy of Congoleum Corporation.*

Changing from basic builder-grade materials to upper-end materials, the cost might run $30 a yard installed. This would give a total price of $420, plus charges for prep work.

Name-brand, no-wax sheet-vinyl flooring can be bought for as little as $4.00 a square yard, and you should be able to install it yourself. Going for the bargain-basement material and doing the work yourself might allow you to install new flooring in the sample kitchen for as little as $75, plus whatever materials might be needed for prep work. Even if you had to install underlayment, your total cost should be under $125.

The problem with cheap vinyl is that in many ways you get what you pay for. Inexpensive vinyl is more difficult to install than expensive vinyl, because it is not as flexible. The finish of cheap vinyl doesn't hold up as well as the finish on more expensive versions of vinyl flooring, and the vinyl may cut or tear more easily than a better grade. of vinyl would.

If you look in a cost-estimating manual for a guesstimate of what this job would cost, you might find figures quoted at more than $1,000—I did. In doing some quick math, I saw where the manual estimated the cost of the vinyl at more than $45 per square yard. The example given in the estimating guide included installing underlayment, but the total cost came out at more than $85 per square yard. While I'm sure you *could* spend this much to replace the vinyl in your kitchen, most people wouldn't.

The figures I have given you are based on my experience and current catalog pricing of materials. There are, of course, some very expensive options available for vinyl flooring, and I assume the cost-estimating manual was dealing with some really fancy materials.

The materials I have estimated are the types found in most homes, ranging from builder-grade mass-production homes to moderately-priced custom homes. The labor estimates in my example are based on actual labor quotes from area contractors, but labor rates could vary significantly.

The cost of replacing the vinyl flooring in your kitchen or bathroom will often be under $500. For this price, the look of new flooring is worthwhile in personal enjoyment and sales appeal, but it still may not be recovered in the sale of your home. When an appraiser checks off the box next to vinyl flooring on an appraisal report, it will not make much difference if the flooring is brand new or just in good condition.

## SQUARE VINYL TILES

Some homeowners prefer square vinyl tiles over sheet-vinyl flooring. Individual vinyl tiles are easier, at least in some ways, to install than sheet-vinyl flooring. This seems to be the biggest reason some homeowners choose square vinyl tiles for do-it-yourself projects.

To get a quick idea of how individual vinyl tiles stack up with sheet vinyl in terms of cost, let's do a fast estimate on the same kitchen described in the last example. You can go to a discount building supply store and buy name-brand, no-wax vinyl squares for less than $1.00 each. This works out to $9.00 a square yard.

In looking at a catalog for this type of store, I found these individual tiles priced at $0.87 each, or $7.83 per square yard. The same catalog, on the same page, had sheet-vinyl flooring, made by the same manufacturer, with a no-wax finish, for $3.73 per square yard. This same catalog also had sheet-vinyl remnants in sizes suitable for small bathrooms at prices of $2.72 per square yard. All of these flooring materials are made by the same company, and all have a no-wax finish.

Based on the figures from the catalog, sheet-vinyl costs about half as much as individual tiles. While technically this is true in the figures given, most sheet vinyl will cost more than $8.00 per square yard. The decision of which type of flooring to buy is largely a matter of personal taste, but sheet-vinyl is more common and a more anticipated type of vinyl flooring. Straying from conforming practices can hurt the value of any improvement investment.

## CERAMIC TILE

Ceramic tile will almost always be worth more on an appraisal report than vinyl flooring. Bathrooms and kitchens both lend themselves to tile floor coverings, and when they have tile floors, their values are generally greater.

If you are planning to replace the old vinyl flooring in your bathroom, you might want to give serious consideration to replacing it with ceramic tile. As you learned earlier, replacing the old flooring with new vinyl is not likely to increase the room's value, but that is not the case with tile. When you replace the old flooring with ceramic tile you are upgrading the room, and its value should reflect the upgrade.

### Can I Install Ceramic Tile Myself?

Is it feasible to install ceramic tile yourself? If you are able to follow instructions and have a patient personality, you can probably do a fine job of installing your own ceramic tile. Installing tile does require precise planning, but the job is not difficult.

### How Much Will it Cost to Tile the Floor?

How much can we figure it will cost to tile the floor in your bathroom? As always, there are numerous options that can affect the cost of any project, but let's look at a sample job and see what it will cost.

The bathroom in our example has an open floor area of 80 square feet. We are going to remove the existing sheet-vinyl flooring and replace it with ceramic tile. The tile in this example is a basic builder-grade, purchased at homeowner prices from a discount building supply store.

As a do-it-yourselfer, this job should cost less than $250, assuming the subfloor is in good condition. The estimated cost includes all materials and the rental of a tile cutter. Not bad for a ceramic tile floor. The value of this job at the time of resale should be equal to or even greater than the initial cost.

Hiring a professional to do the job for you may not pay for itself in the return on your investment, but much of the expense could be recovered. How much will a professional charge to do the job? The tile contractors I normally work with would do this job, including materials, for about $700.

## QUARRY TILE

Quarry tile is very popular in foyers and large rooms, such as country kitchens. To see how much installing this type of tile in your kitchen might cost,

let's compare a quarry-tile job with the sheet-vinyl installation we examined earlier.

The kitchen's open floor space is 120 square feet. The subfloor is not in good shape, and underlayment must be installed. How much will the job cost? At our discount supply store the tile will cost about $120. By the time you buy underlayment, grout mix, spacers, and other materials needed, your total costs may hit $300. You won't use much trim tile, as you might in a bathroom, so the price per square foot is a little less than in the bathroom example.

If you hire a professional to supply and install the materials for your new floor, the price might come in at $960. This works out to a price of $8.00 per square foot. The bathroom floor was $8.75 per square foot, but this was because of the size of the room, obstacles in the room, and trim.

How does quarry tile in a kitchen stack up against sheet vinyl? If you were to do each job yourself, using low-priced materials, the estimated cost difference wouldn't be much, but the value of the tile would be much more than the value of the vinyl.

When professionals install each type of flooring, the tile floor may cost twice as much as a vinyl floor. This is quite a difference, but much of the additional cost is offset in increased value.

If you are willing and able to do the work yourself, replacing vinyl flooring with tile is usually a good use of your time and home-improvement investment.

## HARDWOOD FLOORS

While it would hardly be cost-effective to replace all the carpet in your home with hardwood flooring, it may make sense to install natural wood floors in your formal dining room or living room. Dining rooms are particularly well suited to hardwood flooring. These rooms receive minimal traffic, and wood floors hold up very well in dining rooms.

### Do-it-Yourself or Not?

Homeowners can install their own hardwood flooring, but the job should normally be left to professionals. The work is tricky, and mistakes in sanding and finishing can ruin the wood. Let's look at an example of hiring professionals to install flooring in a dining room with dimensions of 12' X 12'.

Assuming you have removed the old floor covering and the subfloor is ready for the installation of hardwood flooring, a professional installation including materials will probably cost about $1,200.

If you were to buy the materials, rent the necessary tools, and do the job yourself, the cost might be $600. If you are ambitious and can do this job yourself, most of your investment will be reflected in increased value. But if you pay the retail price for professionals to do the job, you aren't likely to get all of your money back when your house is sold.

## Hardwood Tiles

Another option for installing a wood floor involves the use of individual hardwood tiles. Installation of these tiles is easier for the average homeowner to accomplish, and the overall cost is less than that of traditional hardwood flooring.

Comparing the two types of wood flooring, you might find that the cost of materials using wood squares will be under $500, and the cost of a professional installation might be $200 less. While there are some savings to this type of wood flooring, the advantages of traditional hardwood flooring outweigh the minor cost advantages of wood squares.

There are other types of flooring that can be considered, but this chapter has addressed the most common types of flooring found in average homes. Replacing floor coverings does not usually rank high on the list of great pay-back deals, but there are times you can get a new floor without losing your investment. Choosing your jobs carefully and doing the work yourself will make recovering your initial investment a good possibility.

Chapter 12 is right around the corner, and it is going to show you figures for bathroom remodeling. Of all the home improvements you might do, bathroom remodeling should be high on your list of possibilities; it ranks near the top of the list for best pay-back remodeling jobs.

# BATHROOM REMODELING 12

Bathroom remodeling is one of the most cost-effective home improvements that can be done. Second only to kitchen remodeling, bathroom improvements consistently produce strong returns on improvement investments, but that's not all they do. Work done to improve a bathroom can help sell a house, make living in a house more enjoyable, build equity in a house, and produce a strong recovery on the initial investment. Unlike so many home improvements, bathroom remodeling can result in a profit for the homeowner, even if all the physical work is done by contractors.

Statistics on bathroom remodeling all agree that it is one of the best projects that can be done. Some conflict exists among these statistics as to how much of the cost can be recovered when the home is sold, but all reports show bathroom improvements as having strong resale potential.

The recovery rate for bathroom remodeling generally ranges from 50 to 85 percent, but it is possible to recover all of your costs and even turn a profit. Of course, this does not mean that you should run into your bathroom and start ripping out fixtures and flooring. Like any project, each bathroom remodeling must be evaluated on an individual basis. What works for the homeowner across town may not work for you. Before you roll up your sleeves and grab your hammer, do some research. It is always best to hit the books before hitting the nails.

The task of remodeling a bathroom can involve several trades and many options in materials. Since there are so many variables involved with this type of remodeling, it is hard to give generic examples of entire jobs.

Bathroom remodeling can be fast, simple, and relatively inexpensive, or it can be complex, time consuming, and very expensive. You can save a lot of money by doing the work yourself. Even just acting as your own general contractor can save you over $1,000 on an average remodeling job. If you are able to do most of your own work, you can enjoy a remodeled bathroom and an equity gain in your home's value.

There is no shortage of options when it comes to bathroom remodeling. You can keep the job very simple and complete most of it in a weekend, or you can expand the size of the room, install a whirlpool tub, take weeks to complete the job, and spend $10,000.

Let's start our cost-versus-value comparison by looking at some examples of complete jobs. After you get an idea of what a complete job might cost and what it might be worth, we will expand into individual options. We will examine one-piece toilets, pedestal lavatories, whirlpool tubs, full-length vanities, and all sorts of other possible bathroom upgrades.

## SIMPLE HALF-BATH REMODELING JOB

In a simple half-bath remodeling job, there is not a lot of expense. Replacement of the plumbing fixtures can be handled by most homeowners, and replacing the floor covering and light fixtures is not a big job. Painting or papering the walls requires minimal effort, and texturing the ceiling is a minor chore.

Assuming you do all of this work yourself, how much is the job going to cost? As always, the cost will depend on how much you spend for materials, and the cost of bathroom fixtures can cover a wide spectrum of prices. For example, you could pay $60 for a toilet, or you could pay $300 for a toilet. A wall-hung lavatory can be bought for less than $40, and a pedestal lavatory can sell for over $400.

You have already seen some of the cost differences between floor coverings and wallcoverings, and light fixtures can jump from $10 to $100. Mirrors can even vary in price by considerable sums. You must remember how material prices affect the cost of your job, and in some cases the cost of labor. For example, a plumber can install a simple lavatory and faucet in less than an hour, but a pedestal lavatory with designer faucets could take twice as long to install.

In our half-bath remodeling job, we will use builder-grade materials and replace an existing wall-hung lavatory with a vanity and top. The toilet will be a standard two-piece unit, and the floor covering will be sheet vinyl. Fresh paint will be applied to the walls, and the ceiling will be textured. Two light fixtures will be replaced, and the existing mirror will be reused. New shoe molding will be installed to cover the edges of the new flooring. If you provide all the labor, how much do you think this job will cost? It should cost less than $1,000. If you used a new wall-hung lavatory, instead of a vanity and top, the cost might be as little as $750.

Bringing in professionals for all phases of this work could drive up the price considerably. Plan on the price doubling when you act as your own general contractor, and add 20 percent to that figure if you hire a general contractor.

## SIMPLE FULL-BATH REMODELING

Simple full-bath remodeling is a little more expensive than remodeling a half-bath. If part of your plan calls for the replacement of a bathtub or shower, the price will go up quickly. If you stick to the same basic remodeling done in the half-bath example, the cost for a full bath is not going to go up

much. Since the room is larger and the vanity may be larger, you could expect an increase of a few hundred dollars. You may even want to limit your remodeling to cosmetics and leave the existing plumbing fixtures; this gives you a new look with minimal expense (Figure 12-1).

When you elect to replace a bathing unit, the price for materials will normally increase by at least $600. Replacing the bathing unit also increases the amount of time needed to complete the remodel. Walls have to be repaired, more time is spent working on the plumbing, and effort spent getting the old unit out and the new unit in must be factored into the job cost.

A reasonable estimate for materials to do this job yourself would be $1,800. Acting as your own contractor, but not doing any of the physical work, will probably bring the job in around $3,600. Hiring a general contractor to take care of all the details for you might result in a total job cost of $4,300.

When you are able to remodel a full bath for less than $2,000, you can hardly go wrong. Acting as your own general contractor should provide enough savings to offset any loss from the full retail value of the job when you sell your house.

Now that we have seen two average examples of complete bathroom renovation, let's start looking at individual components and how they can affect the value of your remodeling efforts.

## BATHTUBS

Bathtubs contribute a large part of the cost when remodeling a bathroom. If you can remodel the bathroom without removing the bathing unit, you will spend a lot less money. Many times the existing bathtub can remain untouched without detracting from the new improvements, but there are times when the tub is stained or cracked. Under these conditions, you have two options: replace the tub or have it refinished.

### Refinishing a Tub

There are companies that specialize in refinishing plumbing fixtures. If the tub only has only a small crack or stain, it can often be repaired for less than $125. Refinishing the entire fixture will be more expensive, but at least the unit doesn't have to be removed and replaced. The refinishing is done in your home, without disconnecting or removing the bathing unit. In terms of value, having your bathtub refinished may be a much wiser investment than replacing it.

### Replacing a Tub

When you are going to replace a bathtub, you must decide what type of replacement fixture to use. Will you buy a tub that is made of cast iron, fiberglass, or enameled steel? Will the tub be fitted with a surround to allow the use of a shower head? These factors affect your overall cost and value.

A steel tub can be bought at a discount supplier for less than $100, but a cast-iron tub might cost $400. Not only will the cast-iron tub cost four times as much, it may weigh eight times as much. It is not unusual for cast iron tubs to tip the scales in excess of 400 pounds.

When an appraiser puts a value on your newly-remodeled bathroom, the amount assessed will not reflect the extra cost of the cast-iron bathtub. Both tubs will look the same, and they will both serve the same function; therefore, you may lose $300 by selecting a heavy-duty bathtub.

## TUB-WALL KITS

Tub-wall kits make remodeling jobs easier to complete. You can surround a tub with these kits in less than an hour. Compared to the time it would take to install ceramic tile, this is quite a time-saver. The costs for these kits range from as little as $30 to about $300. This is one situation where price often reflects quality. If you install a cheap tub surround, it will not only look cheap, it may fall off the walls in a few hours.

The surrounds I have used for the last twelve years now cost close to $300, but I believe they are worth their price. In all my years of experience with these fiberglass surrounds, I have never had a customer complaint or an installation problem. When these units are installed, they not only look good, they hold up well.

Some of the less expensive units may work fine but I've never used them, so I can't give you any first-hand advice. I know of at least two kits that sell for less than $50 and several priced below $200. I

suspect that some of the ones in the $200 range are worthwhile, but I wouldn't trust the cheap ones.

As for the value of these tub surrounds, if the finished product looks good, there will not be any significant difference in the appraised value between the various types.

## WHIRLPOOL TUBS

Whirlpool tubs (Figure 12-2) are often used to replace standard bathtubs during bathroom remodeling jobs. These tubs can be bought for less than $600, but many models sell for $2,000 or more. This type of improvement may provide enjoyment and better sales appeal, but the cost of a brand-name whirlpool will be hard to recover in resale value.

## ONE-PIECE TOILETS

One-piece toilets are popular due to their streamlined looks, but they are expensive. A builder-grade toilet can be bought at one of the discount suppliers for less than $60, but a one-piece toilet could cost several hundred dollars. The chances of recovering this extra cost in resale value are not good.

## DESIGNER COLORS

Designer colors are attractive and expensive. Most plumbing fixtures that are offered in designer colors cost significantly more than the same fixtures in standard colors. Choosing a standard color, like almond, will result in just as much value as spending twice as much for a designer color.

In fact, some designer colors may actually detract from the value of your bathroom. If the color makes a bold statement, as red might, an appraiser may downgrade the job's value because of the radical shift from conforming colors.

## VANITIES

Vanities are popular in bathrooms and add more value than wall-hung lavatories. It is possible to get a vanity and top for less than $105, but the price might be reflected in the unit's appearance. A standard vanity of average quality will cost about $150 and so will the top. The combination of a good vanity and top should cost between $250 and $300. If the unit is wider than three feet, the cost may jump rapidly.

A modest vanity and top will usually add more value to a bathroom than a wall-hung lavatory, but don't expect to retire on the equity it builds in your home. Double-bowl vanities, gold faucets, and one-piece toilets work well in houses that can support their expense, but average homes will not justify such installations (Figure 12-3).

## PEDESTAL LAVATORIES

Pedestal lavatories are thought of as being an upgrade over common lavatory setups, and they help to create elegant bathrooms (Figure 12-4). Some people, however, prefer vanities; they like having the storage space that a vanity offers.

Pedestal lavatories can be bought for less than $100, but most brands and styles will run at least $250. If the lavatory is set up to use 8-inch-center faucets, the cost of the faucets can be twice that of standard faucets. The combination of an elegant pedestal lavatory and faucet can easily cost $500. This is an expense that is not likely to be recovered if you sell your home.

## FAUCETS

Standard bathroom faucets cost between $50 and $125, but you can buy gold faucets for several thousand dollars. Does anybody really spend $2,500 for a lavatory faucet? I have installed a number of gold faucets in my time as a plumber. Should you spend $2,500 for a faucet? I doubt it; if you have an average house, this kind of expense cannot be justified.

## LIGHT FIXTURES

Will appraisers allow any more value for light fixtures that cost $100 than they would for lights that cost $20? In many cases, the appraised value of a bathroom light is not going to be influenced by the retail price of the fixture. You can spend less than $20 for a nice oak, three-light bar and get just as much value out of your appraisal as you would for spending $100 on a fixture.

## WALL CABINETS AND MIRRORS

Wall cabinets and mirrors are often installed during bathroom remodeling. These accessories are desired and deserved, but be cautious of how much you spend for them. If you buy expensive cabinets and mirrors, you are not likely to recover your investment.

## GENERAL ACCESSORIES

General accessories in a bathroom can include towel rings or racks, toilet-tissue holders, soap dishes, and so on. While at least some of the accessories are expected, there is no need to spend a lot of money for them. Depending on the decor of your room, oak accessories may evoke a feeling of warmth and gather a little more value, but appraisers are not going to look for the price tags on the accessories. It is okay to go with wood accessories, brass accessories, or whatever fits in with your design, but be aware that the extra money you spend for lavish accessories will more than likely be gone for good.

## FLOOR CHOICES

We talked about the pros and cons of floor choices in Chapter 11. Tile should add to the value of your remodeled bathroom; however, sheet-vinyl flooring is perfectly acceptable. If you are able to install the tile yourself, it is a good upgrade, and you shouldn't lose any money from your cash investment.

## WALLS AND CEILINGS

The choices for walls and ceilings were covered in Chapter Eleven. Paint is always acceptable, wallpaper is a safe bet, and tile can enhance the look and value of your bathroom. Few modern bathrooms are built with tile on the walls, but wallpaper is common and would make a good upgrade over paint.

## SKYLIGHTS

Have you ever wished your bathroom had more natural light in it? Is so, a skylight might give you the flood of light you desire. Not all bathrooms are positioned to accept the benefits of skylights, but if you can install one for reasonable cost and labor, the results can be outstanding.

Many real estate professionals agree that the addition of a skylight in a bathroom is well worth the cost. If the skylight is a type that opens, it can help ventilate the room while providing an abundance of natural light.

The prices for skylights run from under $100 for small plastic bubble types to over $1,000 for units that open and have built-in screens and blinds. While spending $1,000 for a skylight would be going overboard for most bathrooms, a more modest unit can get the job done and allow you to recover most of its cost at the time of resale.

## HIDDEN IMPROVEMENTS

When you get into full-scale bathroom remodeling, you might be forced to make some decisions on hidden improvements. What are these improvements? They could include repairing damaged floor joists, replacing sections of pipe, or rectifying any number of problems you didn't know existed until you started opening up your walls and floor.

Fixing these types of problems isn't going to increase the value of your room on a appraisal report, but you should tend to the repairs while you have the bathroom torn apart. If you don't, you may have to tear out some of your new work in the near future to fix what you should have fixed when you first found it.

The only type of home remodeling that tends to overshadow bathroom remodeling is kitchen remodeling. Kitchen remodeling offers all the advantages of bathroom remodeling and perhaps a bit more. To find out more about the battle between cost and value for your remodeling dollar, let's turn to the next chapter and get involved with some work in the kitchen.

Figure 12-1. *This bathroom remodeling job used just a few simple cosmetic touches—wallpaper, draperies, and accessories—to create a great new look. Courtesy of Lis King Public Relations and Curtron.*

Figure 12-2. *Whirlpool tub. Courtesy of Lis King Public Relations and Summitville Tiles.*

Figure 12-3. *Here is a double-bowl vanity, gold faucets, and a one-piece tub in an upscale bathroom. Not for everyone! Courtesy of Mannington resilient floors.*

Figure 12-4. *The pedestal lavatory adds to the elegance of this bathroom. Photo courtesy of Congoleum Corporation.*

# KITCHEN REMODELING 13

Kitchen remodeling must be the king of home improvements. Statistics and real estate professionals rank kitchens as the most important rooms in homes being offered for sale. Statistics also indicate that money invested in kitchen remodeling and improvements is very likely to be recovered at the time of a sale.

Many locations report statistics that show kitchen remodeling can pay for itself and provide a profit for the homeowner, even if the entire job is handed over to a general contractor. This is unusual for home improvements. Many types of improvements can pay for themselves if the homeowner acts as the general contractor, but few can carry their weight when the job is given to a professional general contractor.

Some cities report returns on kitchen remodeling at more than 150 percent. Not all areas do this well, but many report break-even returns or better. Both major and minor kitchen remodeling can pay for itself. If you have to make a choice on only one room to devote your improvement investment to, look at your kitchen first.

The statistics referred to above apply to kitchens that had become outdated and needed remodeling. Obviously, if your kitchen is already modern and in good shape, a major investment is not warranted. But even so, you might benefit from some minor upgrades. Remember, both major and minor kitchen remodeling jobs rank high in projected rates of return.

## THE DIFFERENCE BETWEEN MAJOR AND MINOR KITCHEN REMODELING

What is the difference between major and minor kitchen remodeling? Major kitchen remodeling involves tearing almost everything out of the kitchen and starting from scratch to rebuild it. This means replacing all kitchen cabinets, installing new appliances and countertops, replacing floor and wall coverings, upgrading electrical wiring and plumbing (if necessary), adding storage space and lighting, and a number of other possible options. Major kitchen remodeling can cost three times what minor remodeling would.

Minor remodeling might include re-facing cabinets instead of replacing them, replacing countertops, replacing the kitchen sink, adding a garbage disposer or dishwasher, and other individual improvements.

## CAN I DO MY OWN KITCHEN REMODELING?

Should you attempt your own kitchen remodeling? The chances are good that you can do a substantial part of the work, and if you do, your equity gain will be even greater. Some aspects of major kitchen remodeling might be best left to professionals, but homeowners with some experience in working with their hands can accomplish most, if not all, aspects of kitchen remodeling.

When it comes to installing cabinets and countertops, you will benefit from having help, but the help doesn't have to be a remodeling expert. However, if you undertake major kitchen remodeling on your own, be prepared to be without full kitchen facilities for quite some time. Major work can take months of part-time effort to complete.

Major kitchen remodeling is easiest when the entire kitchen can be gutted and rebuilt. You can, however, do much of the work in phases, to avoid being totally without a kitchen. Taking the job on in segments will prolong the remodeling period and make some aspects of the job more difficult, but it can be done.

## KITCHEN LAYOUT VS. COST OF REMODELING?

Will the layout of your kitchen affect the cost of remodeling? Yes, the kitchen's layout and traffic pattern can have a significant effect on the amount of money required to remodel it. Kitchens come in many shapes, and as we explore the cost of various kitchen remodeling projects many of these shapes will be explained and estimated.

If you change the layout of your kitchen, will it be worth more? Typically, the layout of a kitchen has little bearing on its value. Of course, layout can affect the amount of cabinet and counter space, and this can affect costs and value. There are certainly ways in which altering the layout of your kitchen could increase its value, but reshaping a kitchen is not a guarantee of a higher value. This question will be explained more fully when we get to the sections on costs and values for different kitchen styles.

## SHOULD I DO MAJOR OR MINOR REMODELING?

Which is right for you: major or minor remodeling? The type of remodeling you choose to do should depend upon your goals and what the local real estate market will support. If the only aspect of your kitchen that makes you unhappy is its lack of a dishwasher, then do minor remodeling and install a dishwasher. When your existing kitchen has become such a point of contention with you that cooking is dreaded more than a trip to the dentist, give serious consideration to major remodeling.

Before you embark on large-scale remodeling,

you should do market research on comparable properties. Look to make sure that your intended improvements are not too extravagant for your house and its market competition. There are many ways you could make investments in what you believe to be the safest form of remodeling, only to find out that your improvement decisions were made in haste and will result in financial losses.

Investing $20,000 to substantially remodel a kitchen in a home where surrounding homes have appraised values in the $80,000 range would be a costly mistake. On the other hand, if the homes in your neighborhood commonly sell for $200,000, a $20,000 investment in your kitchen may be a smart move. You must spend time planning your job and justifying the expenses before you make any commitments to do the work. Speaking of expenses, let's start to look at some examples for costs and values when remodeling different types of kitchens.

## SIMPLE KITCHENS

Simple kitchens (Figure 13-1) are kitchens with all their cabinets, counters, and appliances along a single wall. These are generally modest kitchens that involve the least expense to build or remodel. This is the first type of kitchen that we will investigate for costs versus values.

The job we are about to undertake can be done by a skilled homeowner, but some parts of the job may need to be handled by professionals. A homeowner who has strong carpentry skills may not have the ability to work safely with electrical wiring or plumbing. Since kitchen remodeling often involves many types of work, normally done by different trades, it is not uncommon for some parts of the job to be contracted out to others.

This sample job is an example of major kitchen remodeling but on a scale that is affordable. The work addressed is all essential to a functional kitchen in a modern home. Unless you consider a dishwasher a luxury, this job is a basic, bare-bones remodeling job.

### Scope of the Work

What will the work entail? The existing kitchen will be gutted down to the subfloor and finished drywall. Underlayment and new vinyl flooring will be installed. Builder-grade hardwood cabinets will be installed, and the base cabinets will be covered with a stock countertop. Fresh paint will be applied to the walls and ceiling. Appliances to be installed include range with range hood, refrigerator, and dishwasher. A double-bowl, stainless-steel sink and faucet rounds out the bulk of the expense. There will, of course, be some trimwork and other smaller improvements.

### How Long Will it Take?

Gee, this sounds like a lot of work. If I do it myself, how long will it take? Estimating the time it will take for non-professionals to perform a complete kitchen remodeling job is very difficult, since individual skills and motivations vary. In terms of major kitchen remodeling, this job is not very big. To put the job into a visual perspective, the width of the cabinets is only about 10 feet; the remainder of the wall space is taken up by the range and refrigerator.

Professionals should be able to complete this job in a week to ten days, if they are well organized and do kitchen remodeling on a regular basis. If you were to take a two-week vacation from work and dedicate your time to the job, you should be able to complete it. Doing the work in phases, at night and on weekends, you might need a month to finish all aspects of the work.

### What Will it Cost?

If you do all the work yourself, how much will this type of job cost? The materials, including appliances, will probably cost $3,000. Removing existing cabinets, counters, and flooring is a job almost any homeowner can do. If you do the rip-out and act as your own general contractor to have professionals put the kitchen back together, the cost may be $5,500. Hiring a general contractor will likely add $1,000 to your costs.

If your old kitchen is rundown, the value of this job could far exceed its cost, especially if you do the work. Even if you hire a general contractor and pay $6,500 for the job, you should be making a safe investment, assuming the kitchen was in need of renovation.

Taking this same kitchen and upgrading it with better cabinets, a ceramic-tile countertop, more ex-pensive appliances, and general material upgrades could double the cost. Would it be wise to invest twice as much to get a kitchen with these superior products and materials? The increased costs might be justified in some homes and neighborhoods, but in general, sticking with good quality materials and keeping the job simple will result in a better return on your investment than going with top-notch materials and exotic appliances.

## GALLEY KITCHENS

Galley kitchens begin to get more expensive to remodel than kitchens built along a single wall. Galley kitchens have cabinets and countertops on two walls, with open floor space between the walls. Some of these kitchens are open at each end, and some have a plain wall at one end. In either case, all appliances, cabinets, and countertops are confined to two walls.

In this example, we will price the job based on about the same types of materials, appliances, and work described in the earlier example. Each wall containing cabinets and appliances has a length of 12 feet, and the width of the kitchen is 11 feet. While the appliances and plumbing in this kitchen are the same as in the earlier example, there are more cabinets, more countertop, and more flooring.

### Job Cost

The cost of materials and appliances for this job will be about $4,600. Doing your own rip-out work and acting as your own general contractor might result in a cost of $7,500. When a general contractor is hired to handle all of the details, expect a price of about $9,000.

### Value

The value of this job should be solid. The total cost, even if you don't do any of the work, is low enough that it should be recoverable, under average market conditions and assuming the kitchen needed to be remodeled.

You might be interested to know that the estimating guides I have referred to throughout this book present estimates very similar to my own on these jobs. Some of the figures on individual items disagree, but the overall retail cost estimates are very close.

I bring this up to let you know that cost-estimating guides can be valuable to you in determining your costs. In one of the guides on kitchen remodeling, a sink and faucet—described to be similar to the ones used in my estimate—are priced at well over $400. This is about twice the cost I estimated.

One discount supplier that caters to homeowners offers a name-brand faucet and a stainless-steel, double-bowl sink for less than $100. I have used a figure of $200 in my estimate, to allow for a better grade of sink and a little better faucet, but I don't see a need for spending $400 on these items. However, even though the estimating manual and I disagree on the price of a sink and faucet, the total cost of labor and materials for a similar job listed in the manual is less than $25 more than my estimate. The estimate I gave for a simple kitchen is about $200 more than the estimate for a similar job that was described in the cost-estimating manual.

### Compare Prices

This type of comparison is what I advise you to do, prior to doing any work or signing any contracts. Get estimates from contractors and compare them with the figures in cost-estimating manuals. For big jobs, talk with a real estate appraiser to evaluate the probable value of your potential improvement. With this type of comparison, you can draw solid conclusions about cost and value on your own. Since your job won't be exactly like the jobs in this book or in cost manuals, comparisons are the only way to arrive at figures for your specific job.

## L-SHAPED KITCHENS

L-shaped kitchens (Figure 13-2) are very common, and the cost for remodeling them generally falls somewhere in between the costs for remodeling galley kitchens and remodeling simple kitchens.

This cost example will again use similar materials and appliances to those used in the earlier examples. The dimensions for this kitchen are 9' X 12'.

### Job Cost and Value

Materials and appliances to give this kitchen a new look will cost around $3,800. Professional labor to put the kitchen back together again, under your direction, will cost about $2,000. A total retail cost

for the job, if you buy it from a general contractor, is likely to be $7,000.

This kitchen job is well within the limits of rational remodeling costs. The value of the improvement should prove equal to the investment, assuming, of course, that major remodeling was warranted.

## U-SHAPED KITCHENS

U-shaped kitchens are very similar to galley kitchens when comparing the cost of remodeling. Kitchens with a U-shaped layout generally require more countertop and cabinets, but the cost differences are not extreme. Since U-shaped kitchens make use of one end wall for cabinets and counter space, the overall dimensions of the room can be a little smaller. This helps to balance the cost of remodeling between the two types of kitchens.

Dimensions for our sample U-shaped kitchen are 10' X 10'. The cost of materials and appliances for this job should be about $5,000. If we add the cost of professional labor, the total rises to $7,800. Allowing for a professional general contractor, our total will be $9,300.

Getting back to the U-shaped kitchen, this kitchen provides another good example of a remodeling job with good payback potential.

## FINDING QUALITY PROFESSIONAL WORK

Let me stop here to make a point that will pertain to all of these kitchen examples. If you are willing to devote substantial time to seeking out qualified professionals who are willing to work inexpensively, the cost of these jobs could go down drastically. For example, you might find a carpenter who has many years of experience in kitchen remodeling but is struggling to get a new business up and running. This carpenter might provide quality, insured work for a rate that is a fraction of what high-profile, well-established remodelers would charge.

Based on my past experiences, both as one of these hungry contractors and a general contractor seeking out new talent, I know this kitchen could be done by professionals, under a homeowner's supervision, for a labor cost of about two-thirds the figure given in my labor estimate.

My estimates in this book are generally based on rounded-off estimates that I believe will be in the ballpark for many different geographical locations. Using subcontractors I know of here in Maine, I could get this job done, as a general contractor, for no more than $1,650 in labor costs.

Finding good reputable tradespeople, who are properly insured and willing to work for lower rates is time consuming, but you can save a lot of money. However, don't jump to sign a contract induced only by a low price. Low prices are not always bargains; sometimes they are pure trouble. Check all your potential contractors out before making a commitment.

## OTHER TYPES OF KITCHENS

### U-Shaped Kitchen with Breakfast Bar

There are other types of kitchens that you may wish to remodel. A common design incorporates a breakfast bar and overhead cabinets to enclose a U-shaped kitchen. This style requires more cabinets and countertop, but it makes a functional kitchen and casual eating area. The cost of materials to remodel this type of kitchen should be less than $7,500. Professional labor might add $4,000 to the cost, and giving the job to a general contractor may have the price ending up at $13,000.

While the price of this type of kitchen is more than the other types that have been discussed, the breakfast bar and additional cabinets add to the kitchen's value. This type of investment still falls into a range that should be safe.

### Country Kitchen

Country kitchens are typically large and often run into an informal dining area. Due to their size, these kitchens can be quite an undertaking to remodel, in terms of both effort and expense. Usually, the dining area will have to be updated to coincide with the kitchen improvements. Here is a case where you could pay a general contractor $20,000 or more to get the job done. Jobs in this price range can be risky.

It is very possible that spending $20,000 to remodel a country kitchen can be justified, but you should definitely confirm your opinion with that of

professionals before shelling out that kind of money.

### Eating Areas and Other Additions

Creating a light-filled kitchen with a breakfast bar will not be an inexpensive project, but the results can be stunning (Figure 13-3). Expanding a kitchen to include room for a table and chairs is another expensive but effective remodeling tactic (Figure 13-4). Even just installing tile on the walls and new flooring can transform a kitchen (Figure 13-5).

Let's break away from major remodeling projects and look at some of the many components that can be used in minor kitchen remodeling. The list of possibilities for gadgets, gizmos, and have-to-haves is a long one.

## MINOR IMPROVEMENTS

Minor improvements can be as subtle as recaulking the sink or as extensive as refacing the cabinets. Minor improvements, in the context of this book, refer to individual projects that don't require rehabbing the entire kitchen, and there are a lot of them.

Any of the following improvements can add to the value of your kitchen, but don't assume that they will. Before making any sizable investment in your kitchen, compare your house with others in the area. Adding a trash compactor to your kitchen may do next to nothing for the value of your kitchen, but it could bring the kitchen into conformity with the kitchens of comparable homes. The value of any given improvement will depend on your desire for the improvement and how the improvement will fare at the time of resale. Let's start our tour with garbage disposers.

### Garbage Disposers

Garbage disposers have become standard equipment for many modern kitchens. Homeowners with minimal plumbing skills can accomplish the successful installation of garbage disposers, and the improvement can add to the value of your kitchen. If your kitchen wasn't roughed-in with a disposer in mind, a new electrical circuit may need to be run. Some homeowners are competent to do their own electrical wiring, but most should hire licensed electricians to handle the wiring for the disposer.

How much do garbage disposers cost? Most disposer prices range from $50 to $200. Good units can be bought for less than $75. Miscellaneous fittings and supplies will add less than $15 to the costs, unless you need additional electrical wiring. Hiring plumbers and electricians to install the disposer for you will, of course, add to the cost. Here in Maine, a plumber would do the job for about $50, and if a new circuit was needed, an electrician's fee would be in the neighborhood of $125. This means your new disposer could have a total cost of between $65 and $375. This investment should pay for itself in increased value.

## Replacing the Kitchen Faucet

Replacing the kitchen faucet should be within your abilities, but you will probably need to buy a basin wrench. Basin wrenches allow you to loosen and tighten the mounting nuts of the faucets. Kitchen faucet prices range from under $50 to several hundred dollars, but $85 will get you a good one. If you hire a plumber to do this job, expect to pay for between one and two hours' labor. In Maine, this would amount to between $25 and $70. Replacing your kitchen faucet is not going to have any noticeable effect on the value of your kitchen.

## Replacing the Sink and Faucet

Replacing the sink and faucet in a kitchen is a job most homeowners can handle. The options for materials are extensive, but a budget of $200 will pay for the materials normally used by builders and remodelers. A professional plumber will probably charge at least $150 for the labor to do this job, and the labor cost could go over $200. This improvement could add some value to your kitchen, but don't expect too much.

## Adding an Island Cabinet and Counter

Adding an island cabinet and counter can improve the functionality of your kitchen. Of course, your kitchen will have to be large enough to accommodate an island. Be advised, some areas require islands to be equipped with electrical outlets, and this can run your costs up. The ruling on outlets is usually related to the size of the island.

Installing a simple island is not difficult or expensive (Figure 13-6). You should be able to buy and install an island and a countertop for less than $350. This improvement can be worth more than it costs.

Islands with sinks in them are more expensive, due to the plumbing. If you really want to get elaborate, you can install an island with glass doors and an indoor grill (Figure 13-7).

## Under-Cabinet Lighting

Under-cabinet lighting can make working in the kitchen more enjoyable, and it can also make a kitchen much more attractive. This is a project that can range from simple to complex, in terms of the skills needed. You can buy lights that plug into existing outlets and mount under wall cabinets very inexpensively. This type of lighting is no problem for homeowners to install. When more permanent lighting that requires hard-wired connections is used, the cost of the job and the skills required are both elevated.

A general price range for this improvement could run from $40 to $200 for do-it-yourselfers. Involving electricians and hard-wired units could result in costs of more than $500.

Under-cabinet lighting is popular, but avoid spending several hundred dollars on it. Sometimes simple is better, and this is one of those times.

## Refacing Kitchen Cabinets

Refacing kitchen cabinets is a popular and affordable alternative to replacing the cabinets. Most companies say their fees to reface cabinets are half the cost of replacing the cabinets.

Refaced cabinets can look almost as good as replacement cabinets, but the decision between refacing and replacing must be weighed carefully. A discriminating eye can tell the difference between new cabinets and refaced cabinets. The outside appearance of the two types of cabinets may be similar, but the inside of the cabinets provides an experienced eye with all the evidence needed to spot a refacing job.

Refacing is a viable way to improve your kitchen cabinets, but before you commit to this form of remodeling, learn all you can about the process and the expected results. If you feel you will be satisfied with refaced cabinets, you can save a good bit of money.

Homeowners can do their own cabinet refacing, but the job can be tedious. Depending upon your skill levels and personality, you may want to give a lot of thought to hiring a professional to do this job for you.

How much will refacing your cabinets cost? The cost will depend on the number of cabinets you have, the type of refacing you do, and other factors. A ballpark figure of between $1,000 and $1,500 should be close enough for small kitchens.

## Adding Cabinets

Adding cabinets to your kitchen can improve its desirability and value (Figure 13-8). Space may limit what you can do in this area, but if you have room to install more cabinets, you should consider doing so.

Matching new cabinets with old cabinets, however, can be a problem. Remove one of the doors from your existing cabinets and take it with you to pick out your new cabinets. A direct comparison can be made easily when you hold the door next to the finish of the new cabinets.

Component cabinets for the kitchen can cost as little as $35 or as much as several hundred dollars. Shopping several stores is one way to get the best price on your new cabinets. As for value, cabinet space and counter space in kitchens have a strong influence on value, so this type of improvement is usually a good one.

## Kitchen Appliances

When you talk of kitchen appliances, you can be talking about a number of different types of equipment. Refrigerators, ranges, built-in microwave ovens, dishwashers, and trash compactors are only some of the possibilities.

Some kitchens are designed and built with the future addition of accessory appliances anticipated, others are not. If your kitchen wasn't planned and constructed for the future addition of appliances, the amount of work and money required to install add-on appliances is greatly increased. It is much easier to remove a blind panel and slide a dishwasher into a pre-planned location than it is to modify existing base cabinets that were never meant to house a dishwasher. If the cabinets, plumbing, and electrical wiring were not roughed-in for new appliances, the cost of adding them may be prohibitive. Keep this in mind when considering adding appliances.

## Dishwashers

Dishwashers are common kitchen appliances, and most home buyers expect houses to have dishwashers. Of all the add-on appliances available, dishwashers are probably the best bet when trying to recover your remodeling investment.

Prices for dishwashers range from about $240 to about $600. Installing a dishwasher in a pre-planned location is not a big job, but getting one installed in a kitchen where the cabinets were not designed for it can be a nightmare. If the existing cabinets have to be modified to accept a dishwasher, leave the job to professionals and be prepared to pay a pretty penny for the work.

An average dishwasher will carry a total price tag of about $325, if you do the work yourself. Professional installation in a pre-planned location could bring the total price of the job up to $600.

Adding a dishwasher under normal conditions is a good choice for your investment in a home improvement. Major modifications, however, can put the price of installation at a level that is not cost effective.

## Trash Compactors

The popularity of trash compactors varies from location to location. For example, they were popular in the jobs I did in Virginia, but I can't recall ever seeing one in Maine. Before you invest in a trash compactor, make sure they are a desirable appliance in your area.

Trash compactors typically cost between $300 and $400. If you have a pre-planned place to install a compactor, you shouldn't need any professional help, with the possible exception of some assistance from a licensed electrician.

## Under-Cabinet Microwaves

Under-cabinet microwaves are easy to install, and their costs range from under $400 to over $700. This can be a very effective kitchen improvement, and it is one you should be able to do on your own. If you keep your costs around $500, recovering most of your investment shouldn't be much of a problem.

### Indoor Grill Tops

Many up-scale kitchen remodeling jobs include the installation of indoor grill tops. These indoor barbecues are often placed in island units, but they can be installed almost anywhere. Electrical and venting requirements for these units can call for professional help.

Prices for the luxury of being able to cook out indoors start around $500 and go up, sometimes way up. It is easy to spend $1,000 or more, just for the unit. Professional installation can add several hundred dollars to the total cost of installation.

This is an improvement that may not pay for itself; not everyone is willing to pay $1,000 for an indoor grill. Assess comparable properties and the probabilities of resale value in your area before committing to this improvement. Some homes would seem under-equipped without an indoor grill, and other homes could never provide the justification needed for such an expense.

Normal cooktops, ovens, ranges, and refrigerators shouldn't need professional labor for installation. The prices for these appliances range from very little to a lot, but you can check catalogs and stores to price the specific appliances you are interested in.

Replacing an existing cooktop, range, oven, or refrigerator can improve your kitchen, but these improvements are not likely to return their full investment costs.

### Skylights and Garden-Style Windows

Skylights and garden-style windows can let the sun shine in and improve the appearance, use, and value of your kitchen. The cost for either of these improvements can be prohibitive, but when the numbers work, the results are a brighter and better kitchen.

We covered skylights in the last chapter, so let's concentrate on garden windows. These windows can require substantial effort and skill to install. Many homeowners can accomplish the task, but don't underrate the complexity of the job.

Garden windows can cost around $500 or much more. The size of the window, the quality, the brand, and your shopping skills will all be factors in what you pay for a mini-greenhouse. Professional installation fees will depend on existing conditions, but they are not likely to be less than several hundred dollars.

All kitchens can benefit from additional light, and garden windows are good at providing plenty of light. However, not all kitchens and homes can justify the expense of adding such a costly option. If your job can stand the burden of the cost, a garden window should do wonders for your kitchen.

### Gadgets and Gizmos

Gadgets and gizmos round out this chapter. If you put your mind to it, you could probably spend enough money on these items to equal the cost of remodeling a simple kitchen. There are recycling bins, cutlery racks, can openers, wine racks, and dozens of other items that could be lumped into this category.

All you have to do is look through remodeling magazines, catalogs, and building supply stores to find more kitchen add-ons than you would ever imagine exist. Many of these upgrades can enhance your kitchen: both in terms of being user-friendly and in value.

## WORDS TO REMEMBER

Remember this: kitchen remodeling is statistically one of the best ways to spend your home-improvement money, but investing your money in the kitchen doesn't guarantee financial security. Any home improvement can be a winner or a loser; it is critical to assess your personal situation before parting with your money.

With that said, let's move on to Chapter Fourteen and study attic conversions. They offer excellent opportunities for homeowners seeking large improvements.

Figure 13-1. *A simple but effective and functional kitchen design. Courtesy of Azrock Industries, Azrock Floor Products.*

Figure 13-2. *This L-shaped kitchen uses the space well and has an island for even more workspace. Photo courtesy of Congoleum Corporation.*

Figure 13-3. *A light-filled kitchen with breakfast bar. Courtesy of Velux-America, Inc.*

Figure 13-4. *This kitchen has been expanded to allow space for a dining area with a gorgeous view. Photo courtesy of Congoleum Corporation.*

Figure 13-5. *New flooring and a tiled backsplash can make a world of difference to a kitchen. Photo courtesy of Congoleum Corporation.*

Figure 13-6. *A simple but efficient kitchen island. Courtesy of Wood-Mode, Inc.*

Figure 13-7. *A more elegant kitchen island with glass doors on one side and an indoor grill on the other. Courtesy of Quaker Maid.*

Figure 13-8. *Additional cabinets give greater efficiency to this kitchen. Courtesy of Lis King Public Relations and Rutt Custom Kitchens.*

# ATTIC CONVERSIONS 14

Attic conversions can provide a means for gaining extra living space in your home at cost-effective rates. This is not to say that attic conversions are cheap. They are not, but they can produce excellent returns on the investments made in them.

## CAPE COD-STYLE HOMES

Some attics are more conducive to conversion than others. For example, Cape Cod-style homes are ideal candidates for cost-effective conversions. These homes often lend themselves to conversions that create at least two bedrooms, and with the addition of a dormer, a bathroom frequently can be installed between the two bedrooms.

Many builders rough-in plumbing, heating, and electrical provisions for the unfinished attics of Cape Cod-style homes. The expansion potential is so great for the attics that builders assume someone, at some time, will want to create living space in the unfinished area.

If you are fortunate enough to own a Cape Cod that has rough-ins in place, the cost for converting the attic will be much less than it would be for most homes. While the cost will still be substantial, it will produce a strong value for your home.

## HOMES IN OTHER STYLES

Houses that have roofs with low pitches or that are built with engineered roof trusses are not so amenable to attic conversions. It may be necessary to re-move the existing roof structure and replace it with a new design to convert the attics in these homes. The price for these jobs can stagger you, but even with removing the old roof, the cost per square foot for the extra space may be less than building an attached room addition.

Obviously, the cost of converting an attic to living space varies from house to house. Roof designs have much to do with the overall cost of a conversion, and other factors enter into the equation. Still, if you want extra space, the attic is a great place to look for it.

## COSTS

How much will it cost to transform a hollow attic into comfortable living quarters? The costs might range from $7,500 to well over $30,000. Granted, this is a lot of money, but let's take a closer look and see what the reality of the cost versus the value is.

The cost and value of an attic conversion depends largely on how the conversion is done and what is gained from the project. Some good uses of attic space include playrooms for children (Figure 14-1) and bedrooms, both for children (Figure 14-2) and for adults (Figure 14-3).

## THE ESTIMATED VALUE

The estimated value of converted attic space is easier to predict than the cost, but even the value can fluctuate greatly. Some attic conversions will be worth about $25 a square foot, and others will soar up over $50 per square foot. Most conversions fall somewhere in between. Let's look at a sample house and see what value an attic conversion might have on it.

Assume the house being appraised is a Cape Cod. The home currently has two bedrooms and one bathroom. The attic space above the home is adequate to house two bedrooms and a bathroom, and consists of about 740 square feet. What will converting the attic do for the value of the home?

If the upstairs is finished to include two bedrooms and a full bathroom, the space may be worth $18,000 or more. The value will, of course, be relative to comparable homes in the area, but $25 a square foot is a good guess for a conservative figure. It is possible that the value of the home will go up much more, possibly to an increase in value of as much as $37,000. This is a large spread in potential value, so let me share the results of my consultation with a licensed appraiser on the subject.

## The Appraiser's Opinion

When I talked with Jane Furbeck-Owen, a licensed real estate appraiser, I asked her opinion on the value of converting attic space to living space. In general, she was enthusiastic about the idea. Before I go on, be advised, real estate appraisals can vary greatly just within a ten-mile radius, so obviously the information I am about to give you may not be applicable to your home. You will have to consult with a local appraiser to determine the viability of converting your attic to living space.

I asked Jane what the anticipated market value of converted attic space would be on a per-square-foot basis if half an attic were converted to sleeping quarters, without any plumbing facilities in the conversion. Her off-the-top-of-the-head opinion was $25 per square foot. While this was an off-the-cuff answer, Jane is an authority on residential appraisal values; she deals with them daily and is approved by all major lenders in her area.

To give a specific value, it would be necessary for Jane to visit the subject property and conduct extensive research on comparable sales and other factors that might influence the appraised value of the improvement. Since I have to give you these numbers on a hypothetical basis, her figures on this

and other improvements in the book are hypothetical, but they are probably closer to the truth than you might imagine. Jane is a very good appraiser, and she stays abreast of current values, even in rapidly changing markets. Over the last twenty years I have dealt with a lot of appraisers, and I trust Jane's opinions to be the best available.

If we convert half of our sample attic to a bedroom, the value would likely be $9,250 in Brunswick, Maine. Please keep in mind that these numbers could move up or down with market shifts and geographical locations. I stress this point because, as you will soon see if you don't already, there is potentially a lot of money to be made in attic conversions for handy homeowners.

If a full bathroom were added in the attic, Jane indicated the value would probably increase by about $3,300, possibly more. So this would bring the total value up to $12,550, and we haven't even made the maximum utilization of the attic.

You know that the value of the bedroom is $25 per square foot, but what is the value of the bathroom on a square-footage basis? The bathroom is a standard size and contains about 40 square feet. It appraised at $82.50 per square foot. When we combine the bathroom and the bedroom to find an average value per square foot, the number is $30.61.

This conversion doesn't include anything fancy. If it did, and if the luxury were warranted, the value on a square-footage basis could have been much more. For example, just the addition of a good whirlpool tub could have pushed the square-footage value from about $30 to over $36. See how a single item can affect the cost per square foot?

## Cost Per Square Foot

When you are dealing in cost-per-square-foot numbers, the figures can be affected by size, and the result can be a great disparity in the anticipated results. As a builder, I can tell you that the per-square-foot cost of building a house with 1,000 square feet is much higher than building a house of similar style and quality with 2,000 square feet of living space. This becomes a factor in attic conversions, room additions, basement conversions, and some other home improvements.

Why does the cost per square foot go down as the size of the building or conversion is increased?

Many of the fixed costs for a job don't change as the size of the job is expanded. For example, the cost of blueprints, permits, primary plumbing, primary electrical wiring, primary heating service, and so on don't go up much as size is increased.

Many of the most expensive aspects of a job don't increase based on size alone. Taking an attic conversion for example, let's look at some of the costs that will not necessarily change with the size of the conversion.

If you are installing a bathroom in the attic, the cost of the plumbing will be the same whether the attic contains 700 square feet or 1,700 square feet. When the cost of plumbing is spread out over the total square footage, the cost per square foot will be much less in the 1,700 square-foot attic than it would be in the 700 square-foot attic. A bathroom that cost $3,300 in the smaller attic would have a cost per square foot of $4.71 per square foot. In the larger attic, the square-footage cost would be reduced to $1.94. The difference in the per-square-foot cost is dramatic, but you are paying $3,300 for the bathroom in both cases.

Once main electrical circuits are run to the attic, the size of the rooms in the attic will have only a minor impact on the electrical costs.

Upgrading a heating system or running heating to an attic will cost much more on a per-square-foot basis in a small attic than it would in a larger attic.

If you have to install steps to the attic, the steps won't know if they are serving 700 square feet of living space or 1,700 square feet. Again, this is a necessary expense for attics of any size, and the larger the attic, the lower the cost per square foot for the steps. The list of these types of expenses could go on for quite a while, but I'm going to assume you see the point of the example and move on.

While many costs don't change with size, some do. For example, the cost of floor coverings will be in direct proportion to the amount of floor space being covered. Drywall, paint, and other items of this nature are tied to the size of the conversion.

Another factor that influences the value of an attic conversion is the need for space. If you are converting the attic to a studio to carve decoys in, the space may not be worth as much as if your reason was to bring your house into compatibility with other houses in the neighborhood.

Adding space at random will not result in as much value as adding space to meet market demands. This fact alone can contribute considerably to the square-footage value of an addition or conversion project.

## Comparing Costs

Now that you have an idea of the type of value to expect from attic conversions, let's look at what these jobs can cost. Our first example is the Cape Cod mentioned earlier. Assume this house was built to accommodate two bedrooms and a full bathroom in the attic. The job at hand does not require any structural changes or dormer additions. There is 740 square feet of space to work with, and the steps to the attic were installed when the house was built.

In our first look at the cost of a job, we will assume the plumbing, heating, and electrical rough-ins are in the attic but not in their final positions. We will further assume partition walls will need to be built, but all outside walls, subflooring, and insulation are in place.

If you do the work, how much will this job cost? If you shop carefully and thoroughly, the materials should cost less than $7,000. You will spend a lot of nights and weekends on the job; so what will your time be worth in the final value of the project? Using conservative numbers, the likely appraised value of the project is about $20,000. This could mean an equity gain of $13,000 for your time. Not bad, huh? Wait, don't drop the book and pick up a hammer yet, there's more.

What would this job cost if you acted as the general contractor and brought in professionals to do most of the work? A price of $17,000 would not surprise me. Hiring a general contractor to handle the entire job could bring the price of the job right up to the appraised value of $20,000 The prices will, of course, depend on local customs, prices, and economic conditions.

Doing this job on your own should produce a very good equity gain. While you may not pocket $13,000, there is plenty of opportunity with an attic conversion to recover all of your do-it-yourself costs and still turn a profit.

When professionals do most of the work for you, your spread between cost and value is greatly reduced, increasing the risk of your investment. An attic conversion is such a big investment that a professional before-and-after appraisal should be sought before committing to the work. By having your proposed work appraised before it's done, you can make a decision that you will not be disappointed with.

Is it really possible for you to work in your attic and increase your home equity by more than $10,000? Yes, it is, but the cost-versus-value results of your job may not be as good as those in the example above. It is possible that your results will be better, but they could also be worse. Check with a reliable appraiser before spending your money.

The example you have just seen is about as good as it gets. The house in the example was built originally with the intent of having the attic finished at some point. Attics in most houses will not be this easy or inexpensive to finish into living space. Let's look at some additional costs that might have been incurred in our previous example if it had not been so well prepared for conversion.

### A Dormer

A dormer is normally required to get a bathroom installed between the two bedrooms of an average Cape Cod. While many homeowners can manage most of the work described in the earlier example, building a dormer is not a simple task. The work is complex and potentially dangerous.

A gable dormer large enough to accommodate a full bath will require materials that cost about $1,500. When professionals are contracted to build the dormer, the price for labor and materials might reach $2,500. Assigning the job to a general contractor might push the cost up to $4,800. This type of expense can take a sizable bite out of your potential equity gain.

### Subflooring

The cost example we looked at already had subflooring installed. If you had to buy enough plywood to put in your own subflooring, the material could cost as much as $350, and a carpenter might charge between $300 and $400 to install it.

### Insulation

Insulation is another aspect of the earlier job that will not always be where you need it. Some-

times you can relocate and reuse existing insulation, but sometimes you have to buy and install new insulation. This job could add another $600 or $700 to the do-it-yourself cost.

### The Lack of Rough-Ins

The lack of rough-ins for plumbing, HVAC, and electrical could result in some major expenses. The existing electrical panel may not be large enough to handle the increased load of the finished attic. If the existing heating and cooling system is not capable of serving the additional living space, more major expense will be added to the cost of the job. Plumbing codes limit the number of toilets that can be drained into specific pipe sizes, so if your home's sewer is carrying its maximum load of fixture units, more big money will go into the attic conversion. Even when all the primary systems can stand the increase of additional living space, the labor required to get these systems into the attic space can be costly.

Upgrading your electrical service could cost anywhere from $700 to $1,500. Enlarging a home's building sewer could cost over $1,500, and upgrading an HVAC system could run several thousand dollars.

It doesn't take long to see that not all attic conversions are hidden gold mines. Some of them are cave-ins and money pits waiting to happen. You must know how much all your expenses are going to be and how much the new space will appraise for, before you make a decision to convert your attic to living space.

### Shed Dormers

Shed dormers are used to expand attics that otherwise lack the space for extensive conversion. Some of these dormers extend for practically the entire length of the homes they serve. The need for a dormer arises when the existing roof pitch is not adequate to allow a livable ceiling height. Dormers also provide additional width to attics.

If converting your attic will require the construction of a large shed dormer, be prepared for extensive construction costs. The materials for a two-room dormer can cost over $2,500. Professional fees for building this type of dormer are likely to range from $4,000 to $5,000.

## Gable Dormers

Gable dormers are the types normally installed on the front roofs of homes. These dormers have peaked roofs and are usually installed for the primary purpose of allowing window installation. A small gable dormer can cost a do-it-yourselfer about $600. Since a house will normally look funny with only one dormer, if you build one, you are likely to build two. This results in a cost of $1,200 for materials.

Even though window dormers are small, they take time to build, and they can be tricky. Professional installation is likely to run the labor cost of a small gable dormer up over $2,000. So if you have two of them installed on the front of your roof, you could be spending $4,000 or more.

An alternative to gable dormers is the use of roof windows. The combination of roof windows (Figures 14-4 and 14-5) and ventilating skylights can replace the need for dormers that are built only for window installation. Both skylights and roof windows can provide more light than conventional windows (Figure 14-6).

## Roof Trusses

Attics in houses built with engineered roof trusses can be extremely expensive to convert. Unless the trusses are room trusses, it may be necessary to remove the home's roof and rebuild it. Attic storage trusses can sometimes be worked around to keep from removing the roof, but a lot of extra framing will be required within the attic. The costs for these types of work can make an attic conversion impractical.

## SUMMING IT ALL UP

Some attic conversions can produce enviable results, and others can be financial disasters. In terms of resale value, an 80 percent return on the investment of an attic conversion is well within the realm of possibility. For the homeowner who acts as his or her own general contractor, a full recovery of the cash investment is possible. Retail costs for conversions done by professional general contractors can exceed $80 per square foot. Doing the job yourself can result in profits to offset the labor you invest in the job. All in all, attic conversions certainly deserve consideration.

Now, to move from the top of the house to the bottom, let's turn to the next chapter and explore the pros and cons of converting your unfinished basement to finished living space.

Figure 14-1. *An attic playroom—perfect for kids and useful for other purposes later. Courtesy of Velux-America, Inc.*

Figure 14-2. *Attic space converted to a child's bedroom. Photo courtesy of Congoleum Corporation.*

Figure 14-3. *An adult's bedroom in a converted attic. Courtesy of Velux-America, Inc.*

Figure 14-4. *Roof windows add light and a feeling of spaciousness to this house. Courtesy of Velux-America, Inc.*

Figure 14-5. *Ventilating skylights add both light and energy efficiency. Courtesy of Velux-America, Inc.*

Figure 14-6. *Comparison of roof windows and standard windows. Points A, B, and C indicate the percentage of light coming into a room. Under identical conditions, a VELUX Roof Window distributes substantially more light into a room than a dormer window. Courtesy of Velux-America, Inc.*

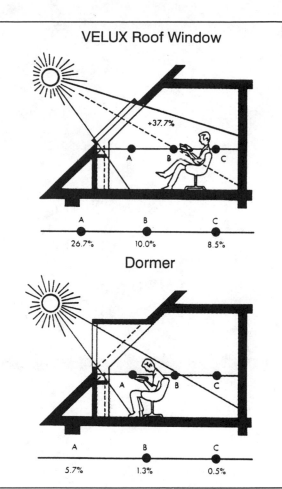

VELUX Roof Window

+37.7%

| A | B | C |
|---|---|---|
| 26.7% | 10.0% | 8.5% |

Dormer

| A | B | C |
|---|---|---|
| 5.7% | 1.3% | 0.5% |

# BASEMENT PROJECTS 15

Basement projects are very popular with home-owners. Many people who would never attempt to convert their attics have no fear of finishing their basements into more comfortable living space. Since basements have floors, walls, and ceiling structures already in place, they are not as intimidating to homeowners looking for remodeling projects.

Dry basements can be converted to living space very economically. In fact, converting a basement is probably the least expensive way to gain additional living space. One of the most popular uses of converted basements is the addition of a family room. Converted basements also contain bedrooms, bathrooms, complete apartments, hobby rooms, laundry rooms, dens, sewing rooms, and other types of rooms.

While a basement conversion is an inexpensive way to gain habitable space, it may not be a wise way to do it. Why wouldn't it make sense to convert your basement? Finished basements don't always fare well on real estate appraisals. The viability of a basement conversion depends heavily on the type of basement you are working with.

## BASEMENT CONSIDERATIONS

If your basement has a full-size door for access to the outside and is equipped with standard-size windows, your conversion can be quite cost-effective and valuable. However, if the basement is surrounded completely by dirt and has only tiny foundation windows, the money you sink into the basement may never be recovered. This is not to say that buried basements should never be converted. Buried basements can produce decent returns on your investment, but you must use different strategies in your remodeling. Before we discuss the costs and values of basement projects, let's identify the three types of basements that will be covered. They are buried basements, daylight basements, and walkout basements.

### Buried Basements

Buried basements are basements that are surrounded by earth and have either no outside entrance or only a bulkhead entrance. These basements typically have very small windows near the top of the walls.

### Daylight Basements

Daylight basements extend up above the finished grade and have windows that are similar in size to the other windows in the home. This type of basement does not have an independent outside entrance, unless maybe it has a bulkhead door.

### Walkout Basements

Walkout basements have at least one wall that is not covered by dirt. This wall allows for the installation of a full-size, normal entry door, and provides the basement with independent access to the outside. Many walkout basements have other walls where full-size windows can be installed.

### Damp Basements

Damp basements are basements that smell musty and develop mold and mildew growth. The walls of these basements may allow moisture to seep in with enough volume to be seen, but the water does not puddle on the floor.

### Wet Basements

Wet basements have more severe water problems, even though the problems may be seasonal. The walls and floors in wet basements allow enough water to enter the area that pumps and drain systems may be required to correct the deficiencies.

## CONVERTING A WALKOUT BASEMENT

Converting a walkout basement to finished living space is a job many homeowners can handle, and the return on the investment is often good. Most walkout basements are already equipped with some windows and an outside entrance. It is relatively easy to add a family room or an office in this type of basement (Figure 15-1). To get a feel for the costs involved in converting this type of basement to living space, we will look at a sample job.

### The Sample Job

The sample job will involve finishing the entire basement area. The size of the basement is 24' X 44'. The existing basement has windows on three of the four walls, and there is a large glass door leading to the outside. The walls are made of poured concrete, and so is the floor. All mechanical work has been installed to allow a normal ceiling installation.

### Scope of the Work

What type of work will be done to the basement? Partition walls will be built to divide the basement into two large rooms. The walls will be furred out and insulated with foam insulation boards before being covered with drywall and painted. The ceiling joists will be hidden with drywall, and the ceiling will be textured. Storage space will be created under the basement stairs, and a standard closet door will be installed for access to the storage.

The concrete floor and basement stairs will be covered with a foam pad and medium-grade carpet. Electrical outlets will be installed along the walls,

and two ceiling lights will be installed. Trimwork will include baseboards, casing around the windows and doors, and a handrail on the stairs. The quality of this job will be equal to the upstairs of the home.

### How Much Will the Job Cost?

How much will this type of job cost? The cost of materials for this job could be as low as $4,400. That's right, only $4,400. Doing this job yourself could result in nice finished living space that cost only $4.17 a square foot. You will be hard pressed to find any other way of gaining so much space at such a low cost.

If you hire professional contractors to do the job, the total cost might be $11,500. A professional general contractor may charge $14,000 for the job. At the price of $14,000, the cost per square foot is $13.26.

### Improvement Value

How much is this improvement worth? Well, the value of the basement conversion will depend on many of the same factors discussed in the section on attic conversions. It is difficult to say what the value per square foot might be, but under conditions like those in the example, a strong return on the investment is possible.

Doing a job like the one described could result in some profits or equity gain. If you do the work yourself, these gains are all but assured. Subcontracting the work yourself should result in at least a break-even situation, under most conditions. Hiring a general contractor increases the cost to a point where you might not recover all of your investment. Again, much of the value must be determined on a local and personal level.

In talking with various appraisers, I've found values, in mid-coast Maine, to range from $10 a square foot to $25 a square foot. Either of these figures allows plenty of room for the do-it-yourselfer to win with this improvement, but installing superior materials or paying high professional fees could result in a loss.

As I suggested with attic conversions, you should spend a few hundred dollars for a before-and-after appraisal before making up your mind to invest a substantial sum of money in finishing your basement.

Another item to keep in mind about this sample

job is that the windows and doors were already installed. If this had not been the case, the cost for the job would have been considerably more. How much more? Well, let's find out.

### Adding Doors and Windows

Let's assume the job will entail the installation of five full-size windows and a terrace door. The cost of these materials, of average quality, might be $1,800. Not only do you have the cost of the windows and door, you have to make holes in the concrete walls. This can be done by renting a special concrete-cutting saw from a tool rental center, but the work is dusty, difficult, noisy, and time consuming.

If you hire a professional to cut the holes, the cost could cause you to faint. Professionals may charge over $1,500 to cut the holes. You can rent a saw and cut them yourself for under $250, but you must be careful of where the cut-out sections fall.

So installing the windows and door yourself will probably add at least $2,000 to your cost. Having professionals cut the holes and install the windows and door may run $4,500. Add these figures to the earlier ones, and see what you come up with.

The do-it-yourself version now costs $6,400 or a little over $6.00 per square foot. Acting as your own general contractor results in a new cost of $16,000 or about $15 a square foot. The full retail price might hit $19,400 or more than $18 a square foot.

If the mechanical systems had to be moved to open up floor space and clear the ceiling, the costs would be even higher. Under these conditions, finishing the basement becomes more risky.

## CONVERTING A BURIED BASEMENT

Converting a buried basement is not nearly as good an investment as converting a walkout basement. The lack of windows and doors has a debilitating effect on the value of a finished basement that is buried in the ground.

None of the appraisers I talked with were willing to give more than $12 a square foot for a buried basement, and most think $10 a foot is a fair value for finished space in a buried basement. Compare this to the cost of having professionals finish a basement, and you can see there is a good chance money will be lost.

The only way to be safe in finishing a buried basement is to do the work yourself. Even so, you must not spend too much for the materials used. Buried basements cause a lot of homeowners to wind up in money traps that cannot be escaped. This is not to say that you shouldn't improve your basement, just do so cautiously. Let's take a look at the cost of putting a large family room in your buried basement.

### Job Costs

What will it cost to put a family room in your basement? The expense will depend on many factors. While it would be difficult to say exactly what the cost of your project would be, it is easy to give you an example of how the job might work out.

Let's assume you are going to finish half of your buried basement into a family room. The dimensions of the room will be 24' X 22'. Your basement steps will be upgraded, and the basement floor will be covered with vinyl tile. Due to low-hanging pipes and wires, the finished ceiling will be made with suspended acoustical tiles.

The exterior walls will be furred out and insulated with rigid foam insulating panels. Light-colored wood paneling will be applied on the walls of the room, and a standard interior door will be installed between the finished room and the remainder of the unfinished basement. Electrical outlets and fixtures will be installed, and the trimwork in the room will be painted.

If you do this work yourself, the job might cost less than $2,500. This works out to about $4.75 per square foot. Subcontracting professionals for the work might give you a total cost of $6,500 or a little over $12 a square foot. Paying for the services of a professional general contractor might result in a total price of $7,800.

### Job Value

How much will your new family room be worth? The value of the room will vary from place to place and will be subject to current market conditions, but a good guess would range between $5,300 and $6,500. This indicates that you shouldn't lose money unless you hire a general contractor to coordinate your job.

## HOW DO DAYLIGHT BASEMENTS COMPARE?

How do daylight basements compare with buried basements and walkout basements when it comes to converting them to finished living space? Daylight basements offer more potential than buried basements and less than walkout basements. Since daylight basements can be fitted with full-size windows, they are more desirable than buried basements. The fact that independent access to the outside, through ordinary doors, is not possible with daylight basements, makes them a little less desirable than walkout basements. However, the lack of an outside entrance does not devastate the potential value of finishing a daylight basement.

Daylight basements are normally equipped with windows when they are built; this helps to minimize the cost of a conversion. You can compare the cost of converting a walkout basement with that of a daylight basement. These basements warrant the use of carpeting and other materials that are of superior quality to what should be installed in a buried basement. The examples given for walkout basements can be used to gauge the cost and value of finishing a daylight basement.

## DAMP BASEMENTS

Damp basements can cause a lot of problems if they are converted to living space without any attention being given to the moisture problems. There are many different ways to combat damp basements. Sometimes all that is needed is a dehumidifier. If the basement walls are seeping moisture, a wall sealant may do the trick. There are a number of solutions to damp basements, and you should find one that works for you before finishing the basement into living space. A damp basement is not going to have much value or sales appeal.

## WET BASEMENTS

Wet basements can suffer only from seasonal problems, but once the basement is converted to living space, it only takes one flooding to ruin much of your work. If you have a basement that is sometimes flooded with water, you should investigate the in-stallation of a perimeter drain and pump station. If you install this type of water-control system yourself, the cost will be less than $500 and the investment of your time will be rewarded in the increased value of your basement. If you plan to convert a wet basement to living space, controlling the risk of water infiltration is not optional.

## BASEMENT BATHROOMS

Basement bathrooms are often more expensive to install than typical bathrooms. Why is this the case? Many basement bathrooms must drain to a sump where the waste is collected and pumped up to the home's building drain. Some homes have plumbing under the basement floor that eliminates the need for a pump, but many don't.

### Cost Effectiveness

Is installing a basement bath cost efficient? Circumstances have much to do with the viability of installing a bathroom in the basement. If the basement is being converted to accommodate bedrooms, a bathroom would certainly be in order. Even if the only room in the basement is a family room, the addition of a powder room would be reasonable.

But will the bathroom return its cost when the home is sold? The resale value of a basement bathroom can be very good if the bathroom is justified, such as in the above examples. If you can muster the plumbing skills needed for this type of job, you can almost guarantee a full return of your investment. However, hiring a high-dollar plumber to install the bath might result in a loss. The loss probably would not amount to much, but it could. Let's look at the costs involved in adding a basement bathroom.

### Adding a Full Basement Bath

Adding a full basement bath will normally only be justified if the basement contains bedrooms. Otherwise, a powder room is a better choice. A full bath is more expensive than a powder room, and appraisers may not see the value to having a full bath in the basement, unless a bedroom or bedrooms are present.

### Job Cost

How much will a full basement bathroom cost? To answer this question, let's look an example. Assume you are installing a bathroom with a toilet, lavatory, and shower in your basement. The size of the bathroom is 5' X 7', and the fixtures are basic builder-grade units. The floor covering will be vinyl tile, and the walls and ceiling will be painted drywall. A sewer pump is required to make the bathroom functional.

The materials for this job could run $2,700. Hiring pros to do the work could more than double the cost, and calling in a general contractor might put the total price at $7,500. If the job is particularly difficult, the cost of professionals might increase.

We know from previous discussions that a full bath may be worth only $3,500. If this holds true, the only way you can avoid losing money on this job is to do it yourself.

## Basement Powder Rooms

Basement powder rooms are common and add to the enjoyment of basement living space. Unfortunately, the value-versus-cost comparison for a powder room is not a lot better than that of a full bath.

The cost of materials for a powder room, under similar conditions to those explained for a full bath, will cost about $2,000. Professional expenses will be a little less, but the cost of a powder room, built by a general contractor, could still hit $5,800.

Since the top value likely to be given to a powder room by an appraiser is $3,000, paying full retail value will almost always result in a financial loss. The cost of a pumping system and the extra labor involved in adding a basement bath is not easy to recover in appraised value. There will be times the improvement will pay for itself, but be careful with this improvement.

## COMMON TRAPS IN BASEMENT CONVERSIONS

There are some common traps in basement conversions that you should be aware of.

- If a basement is capable of accepting windows, install plenty of them. Dark basements are not nearly as well accepted as bright, cheerful basements.

- Many homeowners install paneling in their basements. Paneling is an acceptable wall covering, but keep the color light. Dark wood paneling will make the rooms in your basement appear smaller and less inviting.

- Don't invest a lot of money in a buried basement. Keep the cost of your materials at a minimum when converting buried basements to living space.

- Think twice before paying a contractor to install a basement bath. Evaluate the complete cost of adding a bathroom and ask an appraiser if the improvement will prove worthwhile.

- If possible, provide an outside entrance to your finished basement. Finishing a basement that has walkout potential without installing an exit door is likely to be a regrettable mistake.

- Don't invest money in finishing a basement that may have severe moisture problems or water infiltration. Correct these moisture problems before finishing the basement.

- Avoid putting a large amount of money into your basement until you have talked with appraisers and established the viability of the project.

Regardless of the type of remodeling you are planning, there is a good chance your work will involve plumbing, electrical, and HVAC phases. Some jobs, like room additions, basement conversions, and attic conversions can involve extensive alterations to existing mechanical systems. It may even be necessary to replace an existing system or to install a supplemental system. This type of work can get expensive, and it can also be money spent that is hard to recover. Let's turn now to the next chapter and see how these costs might affect the value of your home improvements.

Figure 15-1. *This basement space was finished to include a home office. Courtesy of Lis King Public Relations and Micarta Laminate.*

# PLUMBING, HEATING, COOLING, AND ELECTRICAL SYSTEMS

# 16

Plumbing, heating, cooling, and electrical system changes are frequent elements of remodeling jobs, and these phases of work can result in lost money. Whether you are replacing your HVAC system with a larger one to accommodate a room addition, or having a new, energy-efficient model installed to lower your utility costs, you could be buying into trouble.

Every home needs serviceable mechanical equipment, but the cost of new equipment is not always represented in increased value of the home. In fact, the value of a house is unlikely to rise much from the installation of a more modern heating system or the replacement of old plumbing pipes.

While upgrading mechanical systems can put potential home buyers at ease and encourage a sale, the appraiser who puts a value on your home may not be as impressed by the new mechanical equipment.

There are two basic reasons for investing home-improvement dollars in mechanical systems: a desire for a better system, or a need to accommodate other home improvements, such as a room addition. Both of these reasons can be practical, but neither may be cost-effective.

This chapter is going to give you estimated costs and estimated values for many types of mechanical changes and improvements. It will also help you read between the lines of energy-saving equipment,

but it is going to do even more. You will see how it may be more cost effective to install electric baseboard heat in your attic conversion than it would be to increase the capacity of your present heating system. One of the examples you will read about reveals how running a new sewer from a room addition may be cheaper than tying the room's new plumbing into the home's existing building drain.

There is a wealth of information in this chapter that can help save you money and open your eyes to various costs and their relationships to values.

## ENERGY-SAVING IMPROVEMENTS

Energy-saving improvements in plumbing, heating, cooling, and electrical work can run the gamut from light bulbs that use less electricity to new heating systems that use less oil. Plumbing systems can be altered to conserve water and use less electricity, oil, or gas to heat water. There are plenty of possible home improvements in these categories that could be considered energy-saving improvements. But are these improvements cost-effective? Some of them are, and some of them are questionable.

Cost effectiveness is a relative term. If you are willing to make an energy-saving investment and wait twenty years to assess its cost effectiveness, the improvement may very well prove to be viable. On the other hand, if the idea is to make an energy-saving investment that will pay for itself in a reasonable period of time or at the time your house is sold, many improvements may fail the test. Determining the average value of these improvements can take some time and research, but answers can be found. Let's look at some real-world examples and see what the facts are.

### Replacing an Oil-Fired Boiler

Replacing an oil-fired boiler is not a cheap proposition, but every year, many homeowners decide to replace their heating systems. Why is this? Many cases involve heating systems that are no longer functioning properly, but a lot of homeowners make this type of improvement to save on their home heating costs.

Obviously, if your heating system is failing, it must be repaired or replaced, and there comes a time when replacement is the wiser of the two choices. But what about the homeowners who scrap a functional heating system for one with a higher efficiency rating. How do they make out in terms of the return on their investment? Let's find out.

### Replacing Your Boiler for Energy Savings

Replacing your boiler for energy savings (Figure 16-1) may pay off if you continue to live in your home for a number of years, but otherwise this improvement may be a financial flop. Let's set up an example and see how the cost versus the return on the investment stacks up.

Assume you have an oil-fired boiler that is old but not an antique. Parts are still readily available for the boiler, and the heating system is not giving you any performance troubles.

When a heating technician comes out to clean your boiler, you are informed that the efficiency rating of the unit is far below what could be achieved with a more modern, energy-efficient boiler. The heating mechanic suggests to you that the old boiler should be replaced. What will you do? A lot of people will decide to have the old boiler replaced. Some consumers will call other heating mechanics for additional opinions. When the homeowners see that the old boiler really does have a low efficiency rating, they will make arrangements for a replacement boiler. Are these homeowners making smart buying decisions? That depends.

### Cost of Replacement

What does it cost to replace an oil-fired boiler? The expense of replacing a boiler depends on many factors: code requirements, sizing requirements, labor rates, and other considerations.

Around Brunswick, Maine, a standard boiler-replacement job will go for between $3,500 and $4,000. Contractors can buy oil-fired boilers for less than $1,200, but some boilers are much more expensive. Since Maine is a state where heating costs can be very high, it should be a good place to consider energy-saving heating systems.

Let's assume that the efficiency rating on the existing boiler we are contemplating replacing is 72 percent. It stands to reason that a boiler working at 72 percent efficiency is costing more to operate than a new energy-saver boiler would. However, it should be noted that even new boilers don't run at 100 percent efficiency, and many new boilers have efficiency ratings in the upper 80's to low 90's.

For the sake of our example, let's assume that replacing the old boiler will improve the system's efficiency by 20 percent: this is a generous assumption. How long will it take for the boiler to repay the $3,500 it costs to install?

In terms of resale value, the new boiler may not be worth much more that the old one. An appraiser might allow a little extra value for the new heating system, but the increase in value would be nowhere near the cost of installation.

In terms of energy-savings, the pay-back period could be quite long. If you assume the home's annual heating expense with the old boiler was $1,500, a 20 percent savings would be $300. Dividing this annual savings into the installation cost of the boiler, it would take between eleven and twelve years to break even on the deal, and by then, the new boiler would be an old boiler.

I am all for saving energy and preserving the environment, but the economical feasibility of this type of home improvement is, at best, questionable. Would you be willing to wait twelve years to break even on this type of investment? Suppose you sold the house in three years, wouldn't you lose money? You probably would, and this type of home improvement requires much thought before money is spent.

### Replacing an Electric Water Heater

Replacing an electric water heater for energy savings may make more sense than replacing a boiler. The cost of water heaters is much lower than that of boilers, and the investment can be recovered more quickly.

From an appraiser's point of view, one type of modern water heater is worth about as much on an appraisal report as another, if the water capacities are similar. Replacing a water heater is not much of a money-making improvement, but if you are going to live in your house for several more years, it may pay for itself.

Water heaters are labeled with estimated fuel-cost stickers. A quick stroll through an aisle of water heaters can show you exactly what expected the annual fuel or electrical usage will cost.

The cost of replacing a standard electric water heater shouldn't cause you to hock the house, and if your existing water heater is old, the improvement can be justified easily. Old water heaters spring leaks and quit working, so replacement on these terms if sensible, and when you factor in energy savings, the improvement makes a lot of sense for homeowners planning to stay in their home for several years.

### How Much Will a New Water Heater Cost?

How much will a new water heater cost? Good electric water heaters can be bought by homeowners, with the necessary fittings, for less than $300. Homeowners with basic plumbing and electrical skills can install most water heaters. A permit from the code enforcement office is often required for water-heater replacement. Having a plumber install a water heater for you will probably cost at least $500 and maybe more.

Before you spend your hard-earned money on devices that are supposed to pay for themselves with energy savings, do some research to make sure the item has the potential to meet your expectations.

## ALTERNATIVE PLUMBING FOR ROOM ADDITIONS

Alternative plumbing for room additions can save you some money. Most plumbing codes restrict sewers with 3-inch diameters to carrying the waste from no more than two toilets. If this is the case in your area, and you are building a room addition with a toilet in it, you could have an expensive problem.

Tying the new plumbing from the addition into the existing building drain of your home could require increasing the pipe size of your existing plumbing. In some cases, you might have to excavate the existing building sewer out in your yard and replace it with a larger pipe. This can obviously get expensive, fast.

There is a possible alternative to all this retrofitting. You might find it would be less expensive to run a 3-inch building sewer from the new addition to a point near where the existing building sewer connects to the main sewer. This could allow you to make a minor modification at the point of connection to increase the size of only a very short section of the existing sewer. This type of creative thinking can reduce your costs and increase your improvement's value.

## REPLACING ELECTRIC HEAT

Depending upon where you live, replacing electric heat with a heating system that is not as expensive to operate might be a good idea. If you live in an area where heat is seldom needed, this type of improvement doesn't make sense, but if you live in Maine, replacing electric heat with hot-water heat may be an excellent idea.

The appraiser with whom I consulted indicated that, in Maine, replacing electric baseboard heat with a boiler and hot-water baseboard heat could pay for itself in resale value. If you decided to pursue this improvement, and if the appraiser's opinion is accurate, you could benefit from lower heating costs and recover all of your improvement investment when your home is sold. This is a good example of a solid way to capitalize on changes to your mechanical systems.

### Cost of Switching Heating Systems

How much would it cost to switch heating systems? Costs vary, but it is possible to give you a good idea of how much it would cost to convert your home from electric baseboard heat to an oil-fired boiler system.

Removing electric baseboard is not a big job, and any cautious homeowner can accomplish this part of the job. The electrical power should be cut off to the heating units before any work is started. After the heating units are removed, remaining wires should be capped with wire nuts and taped for safety.

Installing an entire hot-water heating system is beyond the capabilities of most homeowners; however, if you choose to do the job yourself, the materials for a modest home are likely to cost less than $4,000. This price is based on installing a wall-mounted power vent, to avoid building a flue for the boiler to vent through. Heating professionals would probably charge between $8,000 and $9,500 for this job.

This investment involves substantial expense, and extensive research should be done before deciding to proceed with this improvement. If your investigation reveals encouraging news from local appraisers, as mine did, this could prove to be a very good investment. Not only are you likely, under the right conditions, to recover all of your improvement costs, you will benefit from savings in your utility costs for as long as you reside in the home.

Suppose you replaced the electric heat with an oil-fired, forced-air heating system, how would that work out? The cost of materials for the same house would probably be around $2,200. Professional labor might run the price up to $5,000. While forced-hot-air systems are not as popular in Maine as hot-water systems, other parts of the country are more accepting of forced-air systems.

The same basic principles of value apply to both hot-water and hot-air systems. However, I should note that these estimates are based on homes with one level of living space and adequate room below them to work with the installation of these systems. If you have a two-story home, the conversions will be more difficult and more expensive.

## UPGRADING YOUR ELECTRICAL PANEL

If you have an old 60-amp fuse box, you might be considering upgrading your electrical service to a 100- or 200-amp circuit-breaker system. This is no job for homeowners to take on; only licensed and insured electricians should be engaged for this type of work. High voltage is literally at your fingertips, and one wrong move can be fatal.

### Cost of Upgrading an Electrical Service

How much will upgrading an electric service cost? As with any other improvement, regional costs vary for upgrading electrical services. To have a professional electrician replace an old fuse box with a 100-amp circuit-breaker system will probably cost between $700 and $800. A 200-amp service might raise the cost to $1,500.

### Is This Type of Improvement Wise?

Is this type of improvement a good idea? An upgraded electrical service will be noticed and appreciated by many potential home buyers. From an appraiser's point of view, the new service will add value to your home, but probably not enough to cover the cost of the job.

### Electric Heat Versus Expanding an Existing System

When you are converting a garage or an attic to living space or adding a room addition, you may be faced with a decision between electric heat versus the cost of expanding your existing heating system. Finding the right answer to this dilemma can have a considerable influence on the overall cost and value of your improvement. To explain this more fully, let's look at some examples.

### Garage Conversions

Garage conversions can create turmoil over what to do about heating provisions. If the garage is not attached to the home, the cost of extending the home's existing heating system is not normally cost effective. Then the question becomes one of what type of heat to install in the new living space that used to be the garage.

In many cases, the least expensive alternative is electric baseboard heat. But many people, depending on the location of the job, have a distinct aversion to electric heat. Taking the cheap way out initially may cause you to lose money if you sell your home. On the other hand, if the converted space is a hobby room or will be used infrequently, electric heat may be the best solution to the problem.

Under these conditions you must weigh many factors. How often will the space be used during cold weather? What will the difference in heating costs be between different types of systems? How much money will be saved by installing electric heat? When you begin to answer these questions, you can draw a conclusion as to the best path to take. As in so many other aspects of home improvements, research is the key to success.

While electric heat normally costs much more to operate than other types of heating systems, it is very economical to install. You will have to get estimates for different types of heating systems and evaluate performance and cost ratings. Combining this information with research on market demand and acceptance will guide you to a safe decision.

### Attic Conversions

Attic conversions require heat, and getting some types of heat into an attic is a very expensive task. Since attics can be large, existing heating systems may not have enough capacity to handle the increased heating area. This is another situation where electric heat can provide a solution.

If the rooms in the attics are bedrooms or will see infrequent use, electric heat might be an acceptable alternative to more expensive options. You've seen what it can cost to replace a heating system. Spending $2,500 to install electric heat will be much easier on your remodeling budget than spending $10,000 on a new heating system with the ability to heat all of your home. Not only will the installation cost less, it will take a long time to recover the additional $8,000 in heating costs.

### Room Additions

Room additions fall into the same category as attic conversions and garage conversions. Getting heat to a new addition can be troublesome and ex-

pensive. There are clearly times when electric heat is the best answer to a remodeling situation.

## REPLACING PLUMBING PIPES

Some homeowners believe that replacing plumbing pipes will increase their home's value. Replacing old pipes with new ones will improve the home, but it is not likely to do much for the property's value. Regardless of whether the pipes are drain pipes or water distribution pipes, if they are working satisfactorily, replacing them is most likely a mistake.

Plumbing jobs tend to be expensive, and replacing the water pipes in a home could easily cost over $1,200 and perhaps much more. This is money that could be put to a more profitable use. Avoid investing in upgrades, such as plumbing pipes, that do little for your home's appraised value.

## MECHANICAL SYSTEMS

Mechanical systems are expensive to alter and replace, and the expense is not always warranted. You have seen some of the circumstances where a mechanical system can put a kink in your plans for a remodeling profit or equity gain. These are only some of the ways your job could be affected by plumbing, heating, cooling, and electrical costs. Caution and research are the two watchwords of mechanical-system improvements. In other words, "If it ain't broke, don't fix it."

The next and final chapter addresses many types of improvements. You might say it is a compilation of improvements that many homeowners wonder about but are never quite sure about. If you will turn the page, I think you will find some facts of interest in Chapter Seventeen.

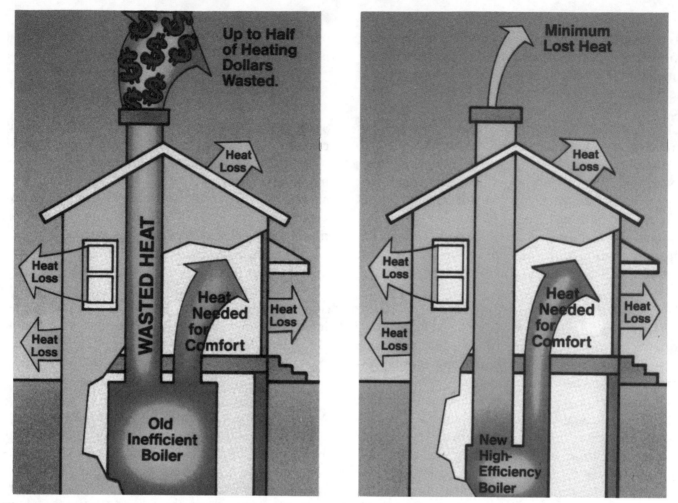

Figure 16-1. *Comparison of an energy-efficient boiler with an old inefficient boiler. Printed with permission of Weil-Mclain/a division of The Marley Co.*

# OTHER IMPROVEMENTS 17

We have covered many of the most productive and common home improvements, but there are still other improvements that may be worth your consideration. It is not unusual for people to envision home improvements as jobs that require carpenters, plumbers, electricians, and heating mechanics, but not all home improvements do. There are many home improvements that involve skills not frequently associated with remodeling or construction. For example, installing a security system is not usually the first thing thought of when home improvements are being discussed, but a home security system is a home improvement.

There are many home improvements that don't always fit the stereotyped mold, and those are the improvements that will be addressed in this chapter. Not all of the improvements in this chapter will be out of the ordinary or highly specialized, but some of them will. All of the jobs in this final chapter could apply to almost any homeowner. So let's jump right into it and see what these projects entail.

## CUTTING A BAY WINDOW

Have you ever thought of cutting a bay window into the side of your home? Bay windows, sometimes called bow windows, can add a whole new dimension to your home. These windows can flood a room with natural light while adding depth and dimension to both the interior and the exterior of the home. Aesthetically, bay windows ride high on the list of preferred home improvements. However, heat loss through these large windows can be a problem.

Choosing a window from a good manufacturer is one way to hedge the odds of excessive heat loss. Buying a window with double glazing will, of course, help with heat loss.

Installing this type of window can be difficult and is not always within the skill levels of average homeowners. If the window is not installed properly, water can leak past the window unit and cause severe damage to the wall where the window is mounted.

Quality bay windows are not cheap, and this can be a deciding factor in whether or not to install such a window in your home. A bay window unit could cost $1,500 or more, and this is a lot of money for a window. Additional materials commonly used in the installation of the unit could run the cost of materials up to $1,800.

If a bay window is being cut into a wall where there has never been a large window opening, professional tradespeople may see fit to charge $1,000 for the job. This fee combined with the cost of materials can place the addition of a bay window in a cost category similar to a bathroom. While the window can do much for the appearance and desirability of your home, it is not likely to rate as highly on an appraisal as a bathroom would.

In terms of value, bay windows are not golden improvements. It is possible that a bay window will add to the value of your home, but the additional value is not likely to equal the cost. There are exceptions to this interpretation of value, but don't expect to see large equity gains from this type of improvement.

## OUTSIDE STORAGE SHEDS

Storage space can be a big problem with little houses, but outside storage sheds can solve the problem. These sheds may be built onto the side of the home, or they may be detached from it. For homes that don't have basements or storage-type attics, sheds can be a good home improvement.

Outside storage space, in moderation, will be noted by appraisers and should increase the value of most homes. Even if a home has a basement, outside storage is nice for lawnmowers, flammable substances, garden hoses, and other items that are best kept out of the home.

The two basic grades of storage sheds are those that are stick-built and those that are made of sectional metal panels. Of the two types, a stick-built shed is preferred by most people. What is the cost difference between metal sheds and wood sheds? How do the two types of sheds compare in resale value? Let's study a couple of examples and see.

### Wood Storage Sheds

Wood storage sheds can be built on site, or they can be purchased as finished units and hauled in on a truck. Either method provides a home with outside storage that is attractive. One advantage to custom building the shed is the ability to match the shed's materials and design with that of the house. The more closely the shed matches the house, the better.

To compare pre-fab sheds with custom-built sheds, we must decide on a common size and basic construction. Let's assume the shed has dimensions of 10' X 12', and is installed on pressure-treated skids. The shed will have stained pine siding and an asphalt-shingle roof. Since most pre-fab sheds don't have windows or skylights, we will not install these items in the custom-built model. However, installing a skylight and window in a storage shed will make it more usable. Okay, this gives us the basics, so let's see how the costs work out.

A pre-fab shed purchased from a leading catalog store will cost about $750. This shed is panel-ized, but some installation is required. A hammer, tape measure, and screwdriver are all that should be required to put this kit together. If you want a floor in this shed, an optional package with the kit will cost about $225. Your total investment in this unit is $975. A similar shed that is fully constructed, including floor, and delivered on a truck will probably cost $1,600 or more.

Custom building the shed at home will not be very difficult, and anyone with modest carpentry skills can manage the chore. Top-notch materials for the job may cost as much as $1,300. Panelized kits are less expensive, but custom building the shed allows you to make it look more like it belongs in your yard.

In terms of value, any of these options are good. If a panelized kit is used and fits the character of your home, it should do fine on an appraisal report. A custom-built shed will not gain much value over a kit model, but how well the shed blends into the overall appearance of your home will have some effect on its value. The sheds that are delivered to you already built can be a bargain, but it depends on how much you pay. While it is convenient to have the shed pre-built, the extra cost may be difficult to recover in terms of resale value.

### Metal Storage Sheds

Metal storage sheds are often used as homes for lawnmowers and similar items. These sheds are inexpensive and don't require much skill to erect, but their construction does require a lot of patience.

Like almost everything else, the quality in metal sheds can vary and so can the costs. An average metal shed with dimensions of 10' X 12' will cost about $400. Putting a floor under the shed will add about $200 to the cost. So for $600 you have dry storage, but the appearance of many metal sheds cheapens a home. Some metal sheds are attractive, but a lot of them don't enhance a home's exterior image. A nice metal shed can add value to a home, but most metal sheds cannot compete with wood sheds when it comes to resale value.

## DISAPPEARING ATTIC STAIRS

Disappearing attic stairs can provide easy access to storage space in an attic. While some people don't like the looks of the stairs in their ceilings, the practical advantages to these stairs usually outweigh the cosmetic disadvantages.

To look at a disappearing attic stairway you might think installing it would be easy. The job is not extremely difficult, but it is likely that you will have to cut at least one ceiling joist and head it off. This isn't a big or bad job, but some homeowners will not feel comfortable severing their ceiling joists.

Homeowners who install their own disappearing attic stairs normally spend about $200 on materials. The price for this job when done by a professional may cost $500.

Installing these stairs in homes with storage-type attics is a good idea. Home buyers and appraisers will take notice of the storage area at the top of the stairs. Some value should be gained from this improvement, but don't expect to get enough extra value to cover the cost of professional installation.

## BUILDING A CLOSET

Building a closet can be an excellent use of your home-improvement money. Closets enjoy very strong returns on their investments, and many handy homeowners can do this complete job on their own.

### How Much Will it Cost to Build a Linen Closet?

How much will it cost to build a linen closet? The cost of materials for an average linen closet will run about $300. Building a linen closet is a small job, but because of finishing the drywall, the job will have to span several days. This shouldn't be a problem if you are doing the job yourself, but it can make the job expensive if you hire professionals. Due to multiple trips to the job, for drywall finishing, the cost of professional installation may run $900. Building your own linen closet should be a break-even or better project. But hiring professionals will probably result in lost money.

### How Much Does it Cost to Build a Clothes Closet?

How much does it cost to build a clothes closet? Adding a modest clothes closet to your home, if you do the work yourself, shouldn't cost more than $350. Having a professional do the work for you

could run the cost up to $1,000 or so.

Both home buyers and appraisers look favorably on closets. Any closet addition, within reason, should be a solid investment, assuming you don't pay too much for it.

## GARAGE DOOR OPENERS

Garage door openers have come to be expected standard equipment in homes that have garages. If you have been thinking of adding a garage door opener to your home, you will be happy to know that your investment should be safe. Garage door openers can be purchased for less than $150, and most homeowners will have little trouble installing the openers.

## CEILING FANS

Ceiling fans (Figure 17-1) are popular home improvements that are practical and pretty. There are many attractive fans available for less than $100. Replacing an existing ceiling light with one of these fans can make your home more comfortable and more valuable.

## INEXPENSIVE HOME SECURITY SYSTEMS

Inexpensive home security systems can add piece of mind and value to your home. Some home security systems are quite expensive, but there are many that are not only affordable, but easily installed by homeowners. Let me give you an example of one of these systems.

There is a system available in Maine for less than $175. This is a wireless system that can be installed by an average homeowner. The system provides seven alarm zones and includes a control console, three window alarms, and a remote control. Extra alarm transmitters cost about $20.

This is not a high-tech infallible security system, but it is a functional system. The value of a security system depends largely on local customs and comparable homes in the area. While having a security system is not likely to increase the value of most homes, some homes would appear naked without one. However, when a security system is considered required equipment, the cost of a system to meet the criteria will be much more than the example given here.

## CENTRAL VACUUM SYSTEMS

Central vacuum systems are a real benefit to some people, especially individuals with limited strength. Central systems are normally installed when a home is being built, but they can be installed after a home is completed. The job is more time consuming and can require some minor modifications here and there, but it can be done.

One-level homes that have either a crawlspace or basement under them are pretty easy to equip with an add-on central vacuum system. Multi-story homes are more difficult to work with: getting the vacuum pipes into the upper levels can require some thought and modification.

### How Much Does a Central Vacuum System Cost?

How much does a central vacuum system cost? A basic kit from one of the larger catalog companies can be purchased for less than $500. On average, $700 is a better budget to allow for a good system, and if the home is large, additional money should be budgeted.

Installing a central vacuum system in a one-level home is a job most any homeowner can handle. If you can install a central system in your home for $700, you should be safe in your investment. Some of the investment may be lost if you sell your home, but much of it can be recovered. Hiring a professional to install the system for you may push the cost to $1,500 or more, and put the price of the improvement too high for an efficient cash recovery.

Figure 17-1. *A ceiling fan, while not a big investment, can add a lot to the ambiance of the appropriate room. Courtesy of Velux-America, Inc.*

# In Closing

We are nearing the end of this book, and in closing, I would like to remind you of a few ways to insure getting the best value out of your home-improvement investments.

Research market conditions and demand for any major improvement you are considering.

Consult real estate brokers and appraisers in your area to determine the market value of large improvements, like room additions, attic conversions, basement conversions, and garages.

Whenever possible, do as much of the work involved in your improvement yourself. Your labor allows you a cushion to absorb losses in retail value, without losing money.

Shop extensively for what you are planning to buy. Whether you are shopping for plumbers or ceiling fans, dedicate enough time to the search to make sure you get the best value available.

Remember that in most cases, buying the best materials will hamper your opportunity to recover your costs. Average materials will do well in appraised values, and they are often much less expensive.

Don't over-improve your home. If you invest too much in home improvements, the cost cannot be recovered when the home is sold.

Keep your home in conformity with market standards. In other words, don't install a tall privacy fence around your home unless other homes in the area are equipped with such fences.

If you are investing in your home with the intent of increasing its value, make decisions based on logic and historical data: not on emotions.

Well, there you have it; we are at the end of the line. You should now have a much better understanding of how retail prices are not always a measure of value when it comes to home improvements. I wish you the best of luck in all your endeavors.

# GLOSSARY

ANNUAL APPRECIATION RATE: The rate at which real estate values increase each year.

APPRAISER: An individual who determines the value of real estate.

ARCHITECTURAL PLANS: Blueprints designed and drawn by an architect.

BAND BOARD: A piece of lumber running the perimeter of a building and attached to the floor joists. Normally a wooden member of a size equal to the attached floor joists and placed on the outside wall end of the floor joists. A band board provides a common place for all floor joists to attach and maintains stability and proper alignment.

BASEBOARD TRIM: A decorative trim placed around the perimeter of interior partitions. Used where floor coverings meet the wall to create a finished and attractive appearance.

BIDS: Prices given by contractors and suppliers for labor and material to be supplied for a job.

BLUEPRINTS: The common name of working plans, a type of plan printed in blue ink and showing all aspects of the construction methods to be used in building and remodeling.

BOILER: A type of heating system, usually designed to provide hot-water heat from baseboard radiation.

BOW WINDOW: A window projecting outward, beyond the siding of a home, and supported by its own foundation or support beams. Sometimes referred to as a bay window.

BREEZE-WAY: A covered, and sometimes enclosed, walkway from one point to another. Commonly used to connect a garage to a house when direct connection isn't feasible or desirable.

BTU: British Thermal Unit; an industry standard in the measurement of the amount of heat needed for an area. One BTU equals the amount of heat required to raise a single pound of water one degree in temperature.

BUILDER GRADE: A trade term meaning a product of average quality and normally found in production-built housing.

CANTILEVER: Refers to a building practice where a wooden frame structure extends beyond the foundation. Cantilevers are created when the floor joists overhang the foundation.

CARPET PAD: The support, generally foam, between the carpet and subfloor or underlayment.

CASEMENT WINDOW: A window with hinges on the outside and a mechanical crank to open and close the window. These windows open outwardly and are typically very energy efficient.

CEILING JOIST: Structural members providing support for a second-story floor and a nailing surface for a ceiling.

CERAMIC TILE: A product used for floors, countertops, wall coverings, and tub-shower surrounds. The most common ceramic tiles are approximately four inches square and are comprised of a pottery-type of material.

CHAIR RAIL: A wooden member of finished trim placed horizontally at a point along a wall where chairs would be likely to come into contact with the wall. Chair rail serves some practical purposes, but is most frequently used as a decorative trim in formal dining rooms.

CIRCUIT BREAKER: The modern equivalent to old-style electrical fuses. These devices add protection from overloaded electrical circuits by shutting down the circuit if it is producing a dangerous electrical current.

CODE ENFORCEMENT OFFICER: An authorized representative of a building code enforcement office. The individual is responsible for the approval or denial of code inspections.

COMMERCIAL GRADE CARPET: Normally a close-weaved and very durable carpet, suitable for heavy traffic and abuse. This carpet is designed for easy cleaning and to handle the most demanding traffic without undue wear.

COMPARABLE SALES BOOK: Generally produced by Multiple Listing Services, these books reflect a history of all closed sales for some period of time. These books are used to determine appraised values of subject properties.

COMPARABLE SALES SHEET: A form used to compile information on real estate activity in an area that allows an accurate appraisal of a property.

COMPETITIVE GRADE FIXTURE: A term referring to an inexpensive fixture, normally found in tract housing or starter homes.

CONCRETE APRON: The section of concrete where a garage floor joins the driveway. Aprons allow for a smooth transition from a lower driveway to an elevated garage floor.

COSMETIC IMPROVEMENTS: Improvements with no structural significance, performed for aesthetic enhancements.

COST APPROACH: An appraisal technique used to determine property values, based on the cost to build the structure.

CRAWLSPACE: The space beneath a house that is surrounded by a foundation.

CROWN MOLDING: A decorative wood trim placed at the top of an interior wall, where the wall meets the ceiling.

CURB APPEAL: A term used in real estate sales referring to the exterior appearance of a property.

DAYLIGHT BASEMENT: A basement with windows allowing natural light to flow into the basement.

DIRECT MARKET EVALUATION APPROACH: An appraisal technique used to determine property value by comparing the subject property to other similar properties. All pertinent features of the subject property are compared to similar properties and financial adjustments are made for differences to establish a value on the subject property. This procedure is also known as the Comparable Sales Approach.

DORMER: A projection built from the slope of a roof allowing additional room height and the opportunity to install windows.

DRYWALL: A term used to describe a type of wall covering made of gypsum.

ELECTRIC HEAT: A trade term referring to electric baseboard heating units attached permanently to the interior wall of a home. Electric heat can utilize other forms of heating equipment, such as a wall-mounted blower unit.

ELECTRICAL SERVICE: A trade term referring to the size and capacity of a home's circuit-breaker or fuse box.

FAIR MARKET VALUE: The estimated value of a property to the buying public in the real estate market.

FINISHED BASEMENT: A basement that has been completed as finished living space. The walls, ceiling, and floor are all completed to an acceptable finished standard. The basement is provided with heat, electrical outlets, lights and switches.

FLOOR JOIST: A structural member used to support the floor of a house. Floor joists span between foundation walls and girders at regular intervals to provide strength and support to the finished floor.

FOOTING: A support, usually concrete, under a foundation that provides a larger base than that of the foundation wall to distribute weight. Footings are placed on solid surfaces and reduce settling and shifting of foundations.

FORCED HOT-AIR FURNACE: A type of heating system that produces heat by forcing warm air through ducts.

FUNCTIONAL OBSOLESCENCE: An appraisal term referring to the absence of common desirable features in the design, layout or construction of a home. A kitchen without cabinets or a modern sink would be a form of functional obsolescence.

GENERAL CONTRACTOR: A contractor responsible for the entire job and the person who coordinates sub-contractors in individual aspects of the job.

GROUND FAULT INTERCEPTOR OUTLET: An electrical outlet that is used primarily in bathrooms. A safety feature in these devices protects against electrical shock.

GROUT: The substance used to fill cracks between tile during the installation process.

HVAC: Heating, Ventilation, and Air Conditioning.

JOINT COMPOUND: Also known as drywall mud, it is the substance used to hide seams and nail or screw heads in the finished walls of a home.

LINEAR FEET: A term used to describe a unit of measure, measuring the distance between two points in a straight line.

LOT NUMBER: A number assigned to a particular piece of property on zoning or subdivision maps.

MARKET ANALYSIS: A study of real estate market conditions used to establish an estimated fair market value for the sale of a home.

NON-CONFORMING: A house or improvement not being similar to surrounding properties in age, size, use, or style. An example would be a one-level Ranch-style house in a neighborhood comprised of two-story Colonial-style homes.

POWDER ROOM: A trade term referring to a room containing only a toilet and lavatory.

RAFTERS: Structural members supporting the roof of a building.

RIP-OUT: A trade term referring to the removal of existing items to allow the installation of new items.

ROUGH-IN: A trade term referring to the installation of material prior to enclosing the stud walls. Examples would be for plumbing, heating, and electrical systems. The bulk of these systems must be installed before the wall coverings are applied: this is considered rough-in work.

SHEET VINYL FLOORING: Also known as resilient sheet goods, these floor coverings are usually available in widths of six, nine, and twelve feet.

SQUARE-FOOT METHOD: An appraisal technique where a value is assigned for each square foot of space contained in a building. This method is reasonably accurate with standard new construction procedures, but is rarely accurate or used in remodeling.

SQUARE YARD: This term is a unit of measure most commonly used in floor coverings. To obtain square yardage, you must take the square footage of an area and divide it by nine.

UNDERLAYMENT: A trade term for a smooth sheet of wood applied between a subfloor and a finished floor.

UNFINISHED BASEMENT: A trade term describing a basement with a concrete floor and unfinished walls and ceiling. There are minimal electrical outlets and little to no heat in an unfinished basement.

# INDEX

# Other Books of Interest

## Home Construction/Repair

The Art of the Stonemason, $14.95

The Complete Guide to Understanding and Caring for Your Home: A Practical Handbook for Knowledgeable Homeowners, $18.95

The Complete Guide to Home Automation, $16.95

The Complete Guide to Home Security: How to Protect Your Family and Home from Harm, $14.95

The Complete Guide to Landscape Design, Renovation, and Maintenance: A Practical Handbook for the Home Landscape Gardener, $14.95

The Complete Guide to Lumber Yards and Home Centers: A Consumer's Guide to Choosing and Using Building Materials and Tools, $14.95

The Complete Guide to Barrier-Free Housing: Convenient Living for the Elderly and the Physically Handicapped, $14.95

The Complete Guide to Decorative Landscaping with Brick and Masonry, $11.95

The Complete Guide to Remodeling Your Basement: How to Create New Living Space the Professional Way, $14.95

The Complete Guide to Painting Your Home: Doing it the Way a Professional Does, Inside and Out, $11.95

The Complete Guide to Home Plumbing Repair and Replacement, $16.95

The Complete Guide to Log & Cedar Homes, $16.95

The Complete Guide to Four-Season Home Maintenance: How to Prevent Costly Problems Before They Occur, $18.95

The Complete Guide to Home Roofing Installation and Maintenance, $14.95

The Complete Guide to Manufactured Housing: The Affordable Alternative to Stick-Built Construction, $14.95

The Complete Guide to Contracting Your Home: A Step-By-Step Guide for Managing Home Construction, 2nd Ed., $18.95

The Complete Guide to Residential Deck Construction: From the Simplest to the Most Sophisticated, $16.95

The Complete Guide to Floors, Walls, and Ceilings: A Comprehensive Do-It-Yourself Handbook, $14.95

Fireplace Designs, $14.95

Get the Most for Your Remodeling Dollar: How to Save Money, Save Time, and Avoid Frustration, $16.95

The Home Buyer's Inspection Guide, $11.95

Home Improvements: What Do They Cost, What Are They Worth?, $16.95

So You Want to Build a House: How to Be Your Own Contractor, $14.95

## Woodworking

The Art of Fine Furniture Building, $16.95

Basic Woodturning Techniques, $14.95

Blizzard's Book of Woodworking, $22.95

The Complete Guide to Restoring and Maintaining Wood Furniture & Cabinets, $19.95

The Good Wood Handbook, $16.95

Make Your Woodworking Pay for Itself, $16.95

Measure Twice, Cut Once, $18.95

Pocket Guide to Wood Finishes, $16.95

The Woodworker's Source Book, $19.95

## Business & Finance

Becoming Financially Sound in an Unsound World, $14.95

Careers in Child Care, $7.95

Cleaning Up for a Living: Everything You Need to Know to Become a Successful Building Service Contractor (2nd Ed.), $12.95

College Funding Made Easy: How to Save for College While Maintaining Eligibility for Financial Aid, $12.95

The Complete Guide to Buying and Selling Real Estate, $9.95

The Complete Guide to Buying Your First Home, $14.95

Doing Business in Asia, $18.95

Export-Import: Everything You and Your Company Need to Know to Compete in World Markets, $12.95

Homemade Money: The Definitive Guide to Success in a Homebased Business, $18.95

How to Make $100,000 a Year in Desktop Publishing, $18.95

How to Sell Your Home When Homes Aren't Selling, $16.95

How to Succeed as a Real Estate Salesperson: A Comprehensive Training Guide, $14.95

The Inventor's Handbook: How to Develop, Protect, & Market Your Invention, 2nd Ed., $12.95

Legal Aspects of Buying, Owning, and Selling a Home, $12.95

Little People: Big Business: A Guide to Successful In-Home Day Care, $7.95

People, Common Sense, and the Small Business, $9.95

Rehab Your Way to Riches: Guide to High Profit/Low Risk Renovation of Residential Property, $14.95

Single Person's Guide to Buying a Home: Why to Do It and How to Do It, $14.95

The Small Business Information Source Book, $7.95

Small Businesses That Grow and Grow and Grow, 2nd Ed., $9.95

Stay Home and Mind Your Own Business, $12.95

The Student Loan Handbook: All About the Stafford Loan Program and Other Forms of Financial Aid, 2nd Ed., $7.95

Success, Common Sense and the Small Business, $11.95

Surviving the Start-Up Years in Your Own Business, $7.95

Tradesmen In Business: A Comprehensive Guide and Handbook for the Skilled Tradesman, $14.95

## Sports/Coaching

Baseball Fathers, Baseball Sons: From Orator Jim to Cal, Barry, and Ken . . . Every One a Player, $13.95

The Complete Guide & Resource to In-Line Skating, $12.95

The Downhill Skiing Handbook, $17.95

Intelligent Doubles: The Sensible Approach to Better Doubles Play, $9.95

Intelligent Tennis, $9.95

The Joy of Walking: More Than Just Exercise, $9.95

The Name of the Game: How Sports Talk Got That Way, $7.95

Never Too Old to Play Tennis . . . And Never Too Old to Start, $12.95

A Parent's Guide to Coaching Football, $7.95

A Parent's Guide to Coaching Baseball, $7.95

A Parent's Guide to Coaching Basketball, $7.95

The Parent's Guide to Coaching Hockey, $8.95

The Parent's Guide to Coaching Skiing, $8.95

A Parent's Guide to Coaching Tennis, $7.95

A Parent's Guide to Coaching Soccer, $7.95

A Practical Self-Defense Guide for Women, $16.95

Spinning: A Complete Guide to the World of Cycling, $14.95

The Scuba Diving Handbook: A Complete Guide to Salt and Fresh Water Diving, $19.95

Underwater Adventures: 50 of the World's Greatest!, $19.95

## Miscellaneous Reference

College Funding Made Easy: How to Save for College While Maintaining Eligibility for Financial Aid, $5.95

Cover Letters That Will Get You the Job You Want, $12.95

The First Whole Rehab Catalog: A Comprehensive Guide to Products and Services for the Physically Disadvantaged, $16.95

How to Handle the News Media, $7.95

The Insider's Guide to Buying a New or Used Car, $9.95

Making the Most of the Temporary Employment Market, $9.95

Research and Writing: A Complete Guide and Handbook, $18.95

Speaking with Confidence: A Guidebook for Public Speakers, $7.95

For a complete catalog of Betterway Books write to the address below. To order, send a check or money order for the price of the book(s). Include $3.00 postage and handling for 1 book, and $1.00 for each additional book. Allow 30 days for delivery.

Betterway Books
1507 Dana Avenue, Cincinnati, Ohio 45207
Credit card orders call TOLL-FREE
1-800-289-0963
Quantities are limited; prices subject to change without notice.